Hear the Cry!

Hear the Cry!

A Latino Pastor
Challenges the Church

Harold J. Recinos

Westminster/John Knox Press
Louisville, Kentucky

© 1989 Harold J. Recinos

Scripture quotations from the Revised Standard Version of the Bible are copyrighted 1946, 1952, © 1971, 1973 by the Division of Christian Education of the National Council of the Churches of Christ in the U.S.A. and are used by permission.

Book design by Gene Harris

First edition

Published by Westminster/John Knox Press
Louisville, Kentucky

PRINTED IN THE UNITED STATES OF AMERICA

9 8 7 6 5 4 3 2 1

Library of Congress Cataloging-in-Publication Data

Recinos, Harold J. (Harold Joseph), 1955–
  Hear the cry! : a Latino pastor challenges the church / Harold J.
Recinos. — 1st ed.
      p.   cm.
  Bibliography: p.
  ISBN 0-664-25035-1 (pbk.)

  1. Church of All Nations (New York, N.Y.)—History. 2. Recinos,
Harold J. (Harold Joseph), 1955–   3. City churches.
4. Sociology, Christian. 5. Church work with Hispanic Americans.
6. New York (N.Y.)—Church history—20th century. I. Title.
BX8481.N5R43 1989
250′ .8968073—dc19   88–17646
                                                              CIP

TO

Rudy,
My brother, who died on a South Bronx street,
Easter 1985

Helen,
My wife, friend, and companion in the struggle
to be faithful to God's justice and love

Jesse,
My son, in whom hope lights the way

and to the memory of
The Reverend Kenneth S. Haines (1936–1988),
whose passion for social justice continues to live on
in those who knew him

Contents

WHERE DID HE GO?

there he goes, a good pastor in
a middle-class church surrounded
by well-cared-for lawns in manicured

neighborhoods just fifteen miles away
from one place that is home to the nation's
poor. it has been a year for him to

speak of the destitute he visited
in all those exotic places
that only the middle-class can reach

with their safe moral outrage, their
passports, and their stories they
will share back home, where they will never

know the smell of the ghetto that waits
just down the street. how many sermons
will he preach about Mozambique, El Salvador,

and all the rest? how many sermons will
he preach about the South Bronx, Harlem, or
el barrio? How many children will he tell of,

dying in Africa? How many has he learned of,
dying on the Lower East Side? there he goes off to
another protest march before the embassy of

yet another unjust government. why will he
not march on city hall, which condemns the
disinherited to the hell of anonymity and

the alleys that the gospel is never allowed to
reach? there he safely goes collecting visa
stamps from country to country. will he wonder

perhaps someday in the distant future how
he spent the time and why he never finally heard
the cries right here . . . ?

Foreword

We North American Christians are beginning to hear the cry of the poor of the Third World, especially in Central America; we have yet to sensitize our ears to that cry as it rises from Third World people in our own land. We are gradually becoming aware of the structures of exploitation and oppression that produce suffering and death in other countries; we have been much slower in perceiving how these same structures operate within our own system. Our interest is growing in the work of the Holy Spirit manifest in the life and witness of the Christian base communities as marginal people read the Bible and respond to the call of the God who "brings down the mighty from their thrones and raises up those of low degree"; we are much less aware of similar stirrings taking place among poor Christians in the United States.

Hear the Cry! offers us a chance to take a much-needed next step, not only in the direction of greater awareness of the situation of ethnic and racial minorities but also toward serious consideration of our responsibility to stand in solidarity with them in their struggle. In this book, Harold Recinos graphically portrays the life-and-death struggle of the Latinos—the fastest-growing and poorest ethnic minority in this country—and the transformation that has occurred in the life and witness of the Church of All Nations, a Latino congregation on the Lower East Side of New York City. The book captures and holds our interest because of the way the author is able to present his case by weaving together his story and the stories of other men and women in the ghetto, by careful analysis of economic and social realities and creative theological reflection, and by his own poetry portraying life in the South Bronx.

If anyone is prepared to tell this story, it is Harold Recinos. At twelve years of age he began living on the streets of the South Bronx and San Juan and continued that life for four years. Befriended by a Presbyterian minister and his family, Recinos succeeded in overcoming his addiction to drugs and became determined to get an education. His brilliant mind and hard work made it possible for him to move quickly through college and seminary, while his sense of a calling to ministry led him to the pastorate of a small and struggling congregation in a depressed neighborhood. As I have had the privilege of getting to know him, I have been impressed not only by his ability to articulate what is happening to his people but also by the fact that he carries the burden of their suffering with him and is committed to their struggle for liberation. I am also impressed by him as a person of faith who has found, through the theology of liberation, a compelling message and a vision of a new church responding dynamically to the needs of Latino people.

I hope this book will be widely read, especially by pastors and lay persons in our mainline churches. If we listen to and ponder what the author has to say, I believe we will find ourselves called to explore new frontiers of relationship and solidarity with the marginal people around us. Here I can only call attention to four dimensions of understanding and action Recinos lays before us in a compelling way in these pages.

1. Deeper insight into what is happening to people south of our borders, which forces increasing numbers to move northward in their search for a decent life. On this point, Recinos compels us to take into account what the "colonial project" of the United States has done to create these conditions. He also helps us to understand how this colonial mentality encourages us to feel superior to poor Latinos, while contributing to the erosion of their national and cultural identity and convincing them that they are inferior.

2. Greater sensitivity to the hopes and fears of Latinos here: their attraction to the American dream as laid before them daily through the media and their anguish when it

is denied to them; their sense of "lostness" in a culture which is not their own, in which they must use a language they may not master; the despair that haunts so many who are locked into the poverty of the ghetto, surrounded by violence and unable to find a way out.

3. Greater appreciation of what the theology of liberation has done and can do to make Christian faith come alive, relate it directly to the struggles of exploited people, energize and empower the poor to struggle for a better life, and re-create the church. In these pages, Recinos speaks movingly of what this has meant for him personally as well as for members of his congregation.

4. A new vision of what the church can become among the most disadvantaged communities of people, as it leads its members to become more involved in the struggle of those around them and to read and study their Bibles. And new hope for the future of the church and the potential for its witness as marginal people take the lead in interpreting the Gospel and making it incarnate in community. In this regard, reflection on the story of what happened in the Church of All Nations can encourage others to undertake similar experiments and provides valuable clues as to how this sort of renewal can take place elsewhere.

What I value most about this book is the fact that its author not only calls us to relate more closely to the Latino people and their struggle but also challenges us to look critically at our own lives, our faith, the churches to which we belong, and our social witness or lack of it. Some of what he has to say may sound harsh or radical, but we would do well to listen closely. For in Latin America, we are discovering that poor and marginal Christians and those who share their struggle are probing new depths of the Gospel message and creating a new quality of life in community. They also offer *us* a gift, as they lead us toward a richer understanding of our faith, a closer walk with God, and a new life of discipleship. Harold Recinos invites us to be open to this possibility here as well.

RICHARD SHAULL
Henry Winters Luce Professor of Economics, Emeritus
Princeton Theological Seminary

PROJECTS

the buildings are falling down around us.
we remember the year of arrival: 1951! the
neighborhood was different. it stood up on
its own and we didn't hate each other, or not
very much, as we recall. our children grew up then

or some of them. a couple of wars took them from
us and dope finished others. we sometimes imagine
the halls in our building without this writing
but in our quiet moments we know the scrawlings must
be saying more than just so many names and curses.

every day the radio news shows teach us to blame
ourselves, and our children who survived the years
wonder why we've died so abruptly. we can only
shrug our shoulders and believe we've told it like
it is or at least like we heard it. we have friends

that moved from here. they're lucky, you see, for
rent control is treating them well where they live
but we know it can't last. experience has told us
what we long to forget—out here nobody cares for us.

we've spent a lifetime in this neighborhood
moving from time to time. it's like serving a
sentence, two years here, three there, and life
somewhere along the road—the last place to turn
we really cannot say. we were hoping you would.

Introduction

Latinos are the invisible members of U.S. society. They are the people who labor for miserable wages in the harvest fields; they keep the country's garment center in New York City moving; they work in the kitchens of fancy restaurants; they empty the computer print from the trash bins on Wall Street and in the World Bank office building in the nation's capital. Latinos are condemned to live out their lives in the new "cotton fields" of Latin America; they are turned away when they try to come to that one great country that is home to the world's symbol of compassion, freedom, and justice—the Statue of Liberty. The Latino poor in the United States suffer human disfigurement each day because of the oppressive weight of racial discrimination, disadvantage, and economic injustice. Their lives depict the existential reality of Golgotha, echoing the cry of the cross, "My God, my God, why hast thou forsaken me?" Their cry is heard by the God who stands beside those who feel totally abandoned. The cross of Jesus of Nazareth means that Latino invisibility is being overcome.

The Lower East Side of Manhattan is home to a variety of ethnic groups. The Puerto Rican community constitutes a majority within a collection of mostly Eastern European, Jewish, and Anglo-American people. Puerto Ricans on the Lower East Side are either members of the working poor, underemployed, or chronically unemployed. Their story is seldom told in the media. This silence surrounding the Puerto Rican community has been partly responsible for the wretched conditions in which many Puerto Ricans live. The church must exercise its transforming role by incarnating itself in the lives of these persons, who are crushed daily by the vicious cycles of poverty and oppression.

The Church of All Nations was established in 1955. The first pastor was a Cuban expatriate with strong conservative evangelical perceptions of religion and politics. She served the congregation for some nineteen years. A strong sense of anticommunism was nurtured during that time. Privatized Christianity was harmonized with conservative thinking, which resulted in a false dichotomy between the world and the so-called "sanctified community." Evangelism was a top priority on the first pastor's agenda. However, evangelism meant saving souls for Jesus. Understanding the existing situation of oppression suffered by the Latino community was not an element of the mission of the church. "Jesus saves" was the magic formula used to give psychological consolation to suffering humanity. Yet, by and large, it did not change the reality of the family members facing eviction from their apartment, the child in jail for being Puerto Rican, the daughter addicted to dope and walking the street as a prostitute, the lack of jobs in the Latino community, or the high rate of high school dropouts. The conservative evangelical formula "Jesus saves" failed to include concern for social and institutional redemption.

When I came to serve the Church of All Nations in 1981, the congregation was no longer able to reconcile this ahistorical faith with the reality it was experiencing. The old traditional formula was not helping to realize the kingdom of God in the life of the poor on the Lower East Side. The magic was just not working. The Church of All Nations thought it imperative to begin a new journey with the help of social analysis and liberation theology. What does it mean to call oneself a follower of Jesus Christ in the context of a community suffering human disfigurement and spiritual despair? How does one small church begin to embody the prophetic spirit of scripture and speak on behalf of the voiceless? What is the relationship between the Christian understanding of *kenosis* (self-emptying; Phil. 2:5–7) and the poor? These are some of the questions that motivated the study and actions of the Church of All Nations over a two-year period. The success of the project depended on the openness and vulnerability of each of the participants. Breaking with some fundamental faith postures naturally created a certain degree of tension, but the promise of a renewed faith perspective dispelled all fear.

I would like to thank the faculty of New York Theological Seminary for its help and advice; the seminary peer team for reading my material; Dr. Charles T. Yerkes for his contributions; the local church site team, consisting of Bienvenida Aguila, Judy Aguila, Annabelle Cabrera, Jesse Cabrera, Jesus Cabrera, Esther Castillo, Pedro Cohn, Maria Feliciano, Angela Martinez, Carlos Rodriguez, Joseph Sotomayor, and Librada Sotomayor for their support; the homesteaders of the Lower East Side for bringing the housing issue to the church's attention; the Center for Immigrants' Rights for its contributions to the project; the editors of Westminster/John Knox Press; and my wife, Helen, for her support and encouragement.

HEROIN SYMPTOMS

the symptoms the symptoms the symptoms:
standing on corners squatting on rooftops
with needles imbedded in leatherlike tracks.

the symptoms the symptoms the symptoms:
falling upon prey, never ceasing to surprise,
knives smoothly entering through skin

proclaiming yet another rape. the symptoms
the symptoms the symptoms: it's junkie paradise
this hell where death is dealt in dime bags

beneath streetlights that come on at dusk.
it's forgotten mothers on welfare lines deciding
what next, the crooked life; it's fathers in

junkie masks still not knowing the name
of the last strung-out child sired. the
symptoms the symptoms the symptoms: they

are everywhere, beneath the stairwells,
in fancy offices leaning forward, peering,
through windows in buildings that will never rest,

left there by those now living out of town.
the symptoms the symptoms the symptoms: directed
and nodding out. . . .

1

Journey
to Wholeness

In the weeks following my appointment as pastor to the Church of All Nations in 1981, I came to understand clearly what kind of faith journey that parish would have to take. Faith had always been understood by most in the congregation in strictly private terms. The parish's new journey would involve finding a way to overcome the tendency to escape from the world through private Christianity.

The struggle to live out a spirituality of engagement was actually not foreign to my own personal experience. In my youth I had encountered privatized fundamentalist Christianity in mostly negative ways. I lived on the streets of New York City, Los Angeles, and Old San Juan from age twelve to age sixteen. I made my home in condemned tenements, parked buses, local parks, and Bowery-style mission houses. I never entered the life of crime; instead, I learned to beg for money. I was a junkie. My life on the streets was devoted to the daily struggle of getting a fix: the bondage of heroin, the painful isolation of addiction. The needle that dangled from my veins several times a day was comfort and companionship.

Evangelical Christians standing on the corner in the South Bronx are a common sight. Street preachers can be found on any given day decrying sinfulness to empty streets. The audiences they command are the condemned buildings, stray hungry dogs that dig through garbage, and a small following of family and friends. I never doubted that Jesus has the power to save—my strong Catholic back-

ground made that understanding second nature—but that
power to save was otherworldly. The street preachers had
the right idea about Jesus saving in this life, but they
tended to blame the victims of injustice. I did not believe
that by demanding a change in the behavior of the oppressed, all would be well in the South Bronx. Emotional
optimism over a concept like "Jesus saves" was not possible for me when I knew that Wall Street business persons
were divesting South Bronx real estate and investing in
dope. The Puerto Rican poor who lived there needed
Jesus to save them from the sinful practices of corporate
and private economic greed that condemned many families to the wretched abandonment of Golgotha.

In 1968 I used to sleep in a hotel located on Thirty-
eighth Street in Manhattan. The rooms rented for $3.75
per night. I was thirteen years old at the time, and nobody
ever questioned me as I registered for a room. Why should
the desk manager ask questions? Society's outcasts were
the only guests in that hotel: junkies, queers, transvestites,
muggers, winos, hookers, murderers, elderly poor, and
white trash. The hotel corridors were always filled with
the night cries of queers, fights between hookers and
pimps, and the sound of wine bottles breaking on the cold
tile floor. My nights were filled with anxiety that someone
would break into the room. As I lay awake one evening,
staring at the electric wire from which a light bulb dangled precariously above the bed, I decided to go west.

The Trip West

I treated myself to a last shot of heroin before heading
for the bus station at the Port Authority Building. I had
decided to travel to Southern California by bus, conclud-
ing that the long trip would allow enough time to kick my
addiction. I purchased a bus ticket with money raised by
begging on the streets. Naturally, the first twenty-four
hours on the bus were easy to handle, given all the dope
in my circulatory system. I was feeling very relaxed, but
I knew the withdrawal symptoms would take hold soon,

putting knots in my stomach. My skin would feel clammy, cold sweats and diarrhea would dominate my body, and a sense of desperation would color my perceptions.

Once the high was gone I felt as though someone had tied my stomach up with copper wire. I was running back and forth to the bathroom at the rear of the bus. I am sure the other passengers began to wonder about my ailment. The bus would be stopping in St. Louis for approximately two hours. All I could think of was finding a junkie there to buy some dope for me. The bus station in St. Louis was located beside a low-income housing project. The two-hour rest period would give me just enough time. I should have known better than to enter the project, a complete stranger to the area, and expect somebody to buy dope for me. A sick junkie will try anything that offers the possibility of an immediate fix.

I discovered a St. Louis "dope fiend" standing outside a candy store, drinking from a bottle of wine hidden inside a brown paper bag. I walked over and explained my desperation to him. I offered to pay him twenty dollars extra if he would buy a ten-dollar bag of dope for me. "Give me all the money now. You can trust me, man! I won't beat you for your money. I know you're sick, bro!" I gave him all the money, and I waited for a long time in front of that candy store for my trustworthy "friend" to return with the fix. Of course, he never came back. I returned to the bus station thirty dollars poorer and sicker than ever.

I got back just in time to make the bus connection. My clothing was starting to smell from all the sweating associated with withdrawal. I also had had a minor accident in my pants, so I washed them in the bathroom basin. I did not own a change of clothing. One consolation to the trip was that no one wished to sit next to me. I was able to spread out in my section of seats. Junkies bear a disease of social isolation. No one on the bus wanted to get next to a sick thirteen-year-old to provide comfort. I was all alone and without dope.

When the bus arrived in Los Angeles some days later, I was starting to feel a great deal better. My thoughts were still dominated by the compulsion to get a fix, however. The very first thing I did was to search for a junkie in the local ghetto. I was far more successful at accomplishing my goal of getting a fix this time around. I visited a shooting gallery (a place where junkies share needles and get high). Puerto Ricans and Dominicans were killing themselves on the East Coast with dope; on the West Coast, Chicanos and Central Americans were the victims. Dope had become the answer to our common experience of social wretchedness. In Los Angeles, I realized the depth of my own anger at the structure of a world that denied me a family and substituted shooting galleries. My interior life was numbed by wounds borne at such an early age. The experience of so much loss and social isolation caused me to question the idea of a loving God. How could a loving God exist and permit so much pain and suffering in my life? What did I do to deserve all that I was experiencing? I began to roam the beaches outside of Los Angeles, especially Newport Beach and the town of Santa Ana.

I became a "high-class" street person in Newport Beach. A group of North American college-age youths living in Newport Beach befriended me. It was now 1969. The civil rights protests in the country had evolved into the peace movement. The youths I met were reacting negatively to the values of their wealthy parents. They all expressed a strong objection to becoming a part of the establishment. One friend had created an elaborate fantasy about going to New Zealand to become a world-renowned chess master in the tradition of Bobby Fischer. I thought life in the South Bronx was bad! My perception of the world was at a much higher level of maturity than that of most of my Newport Beach friends. Their sense of reality was very distorted. They would never have to serve on the front lines in Vietnam, given their families' influence. My friends in the South Bronx were being sent to die in order to permit this Newport Beach crowd to stay in the States and indulge their antiestablishment delusions. The rent on the exclusive beach homes in which these friends lived was being paid by parents willing to tolerate late-adolescent rebellion. My friends in Newport Beach were unwilling and unable truly to give up the privilege of their class.

I had always dreamed of returning to school. After I left home over an argument and found myself living on the streets, it became impossible to pursue an education. My attempt to enter high school in California turned out to be futile. It was necessary to be a legal resident of the state and have a guardian to enter school. The barriers I ran up against in California made me very restless. I had managed to stop shooting dope, but the lack of any sense of a positive future was pushing me in the direction of addiction again. All the signs indicated it was time to say good-bye to my Newport Beach friends and move on to some other place that offered the promise of a real life. I decided to travel to Puerto Rico to search for my identity. My family had come from there. I was able to project all my feelings for family onto the island. Puerto Rico became my mythological home. I raised enough money to buy a plane ticket to the island of enchantment and bid farewell to my friends. I knew I would never see them again.

Winter in Puerto Rico

The flight made a scheduled stop in New York City to drop off and pick up passengers. The thought of staying in New York crossed my mind, but only condemned tenements awaited me. The tropical beaches of San Juan seemed a more comforting image in February than a heatless abandoned tenement in New York City. The needle would make its way into my life very fast in New York. After evaluating the choices, I decided to go on to Puerto Rico. What is Puerto Rico like? I wondered. I had family in Santurce I had never met. My older brother, Rudy, was living with the Betancourts in the little town of Carolina. I was very excited about the adventures that awaited me on the island, although I had no idea of what would really happen.

Most of the people on the plane were Puerto Ricans living in New York who were on the way to visit family.

The flight down was festive, with people conversing happily about family, friends, and the island's beauty in winter. The man in the next seat bought me a rum and Coke. Five hours later, the plane began its descent for landing at the San Juan International Airport. I was slightly drunk from the rum and Coke and the excitement of getting to experience Puerto Rico at first hand.

My immediate impression of the island was very confused. I had expected to find signs of a completely independent culture, but North American consumerism was dominant. Billboards advertising American products lined the highway leading to Old San Juan. The description of colonial society I had heard in the South Bronx took on meaning for me: Puerto Rico imports what it does not need and exports what it most requires. The island has a dependent economy from which most of the population has been displaced. The people of Puerto Rico cannot even boast of owning an independent major commercial airline to serve the tourist industry. The airline business is all in the hands of North American or foreign corporations. Puerto Rico is a barrio with palm trees.

I boarded a bus for Old San Juan. Its route followed the coastline from the airport to the colonial city. It passed the exclusive tourist district located in Condado. The Spanish colonizers built the city of Old San Juan some four hundred years ago. The island served as a military outpost of Spain for the first two hundred years of its history following the conquest. The Spaniards constructed two huge forts in Old San Juan to defend against invasion: one fort faces the ocean, the other the harbor. I lived in a park named after Christopher Columbus, La Plaza de Colón, which was just across the street from the fort also bearing his name. A small shantytown community had been constructed by the poor in the coastal area separating those two monuments to the Iberian colonial past. The community is known to most islanders by the name of La Perla: the Pearl. Tourists are warned against walking there alone at any time of day or night. I returned to the junkie life in that plywood community.

I was tired of loneliness. I was searching for a place to call home, someone for conversation and company. Despite the fact that I was a minor in Puerto Rico, one bar served me drinks, and I visited it regularly. My hangovers became too difficult to handle and forced me to stop going to the bar. The park benches were starting to feel very uncomfortable, but I discovered a mission house that offered dormitory-like accommodations for $1.50 per night. My level of frustration was increasing, pushing me to the comfort of the needle.

The flophouse had a Mediterranean atmosphere. Army-surplus beds lined all the available space of the huge gymnasium-like room. A sea of despised humanity filled the place with the sounds of arguments, coughing, groans, and cigarette smoke. I learned to sit at the edge of my cot like the others, blowing smoke toward the ceiling in a mindless state. The room trembled whenever cars drove by in front of the building. Life was without hope there. I can still remember the face of the old man occupying the cot next to mine. A long cigar was pinched between his teeth. His week-long beard covered a scarred face that kept appearing and disappearing behind the cloud of cigar smoke.

One afternoon, I went for a walk down one of the side streets of the old city and came across a Salvation Army boardinghouse. The woman in charge of the mission was named Maria. She seemed a sympathetic person who might listen to my story. I explained that the town square was my home and I had no family to take care of me. Maria felt compassion for me. She was one of the few Christian evangelicals I met who responded with both concrete action and effective love. The Salvation Army has a long history of coming to the aid of people who are not easily recognized by status quo institutions. Maria invited me to live at the boardinghouse. She placed me in a room with three other persons: a mentally ill man, a merchant seaman who had missed his ship following a night out on the town, and an older man suffering from liver disease. The seaman complained daily about missing the Mardi Gras celebrations being held in his hometown, New Orleans. I attempted to console him by saying, "Don't worry about it. You'll make the next one."

I was able to earn a little money doing odd jobs around Old San Juan. The money would help to buy a plane ticket back to New York at some future date. The year that had just passed for me outside of New York was finally turning into an experience of homesickness. Spring would be the best time to migrate back to the Big Apple.

Life in Puerto Rico was not very satisfying. My daily morning ritual consisted of going out on the Salvation Army truck to gather clothing donated by middle-class families for distribution to the poor and needy. In the afternoons I roamed the old city, feeling quite empty, especially as I watched tourists from the States with children my own age sharing the family experience. My consolation was to go back to shooting heroin. The old city was full of junkies roaming the streets, hoping to hustle money from tourists. I met one junkie named Tito. He was extremely muscle-bound. He had the kind of muscle put on by junkies who have spent time behind bars. Tito's physical development indicated a jail stay of no less than a year. His arms gave him away on the spot. I had never seen tracks or needle scars that long. They ran from the top of his biceps to the middle of his hand. We talked for a few minutes in the park; then I followed Tito into the shantytown to buy dope from one of his connections.

We followed the long hill that empties into a large alleyway of La Perla. Automobiles never entered most of the small streets in the shantytown community because the shelters were constructed so close together. The design of each shack was determined by the available building material. Running water or bathroom facilities were not common features in any of the homes in La Perla. Waste was discarded in the ocean nearby. Water was collected from one of the fire hydrants out on the road. I followed Tito through an intricate system of alleys winding through the community until we reached the home of his connection. The business was all transacted through a small hole in the shack door. An anonymous person on the other side of the door took the money and returned with the bags of dope.

We made our way once again through the alleyways to the home of an old-timer who rented "works" (needles) to junkies for a dollar. The man who answered the door was missing a leg. He escorted us to a room used both as a shooting gallery and a chicken house. Chicken dirt covered the sandy floor, forcing us to pay attention to each step. Sunlight filtered into the room through the uneven wood slats that served as walls. It was very hot. The chickens were excited to have visitors. All I wanted to do was shoot up the dope and forget about being alone. I made many other trips to La Perla following that visit, mostly alone. Tito was no longer useful to me. A junkie hates to share his dope.

My habit never got out of hand in Puerto Rico, although I did steal a typewriter from the Salvation Army to buy dope one desperate afternoon. I didn't want to spend any of the money I had saved for my ticket back to the States. My guilt over the incident caused me to work doubly hard when the truck went out to collect clothing. Whenever I returned to the boardinghouse, I would check to see if I had sufficient funds for a plane ride to the Big Apple. One day I found I had enough to buy a ticket, but only to Miami, Florida. It was a disappointing revelation, but not the end of the world. I would simply fly to Miami and hitchhike the rest of the way.

I went to tell Maria of my decision. "I am going back to New York City, Maria. *Gracias por todo.* Thanks for everything." We sat together and cried for a few minutes. She was the closest thing to a mother I had ever known in all my time on the streets. I will never forget her.

Florida

I arrived at Miami's International Airport with about ten dollars to my name. All I had were the clothes on my back. I took the bus for downtown Miami Beach, intending to find a quiet place to sleep before starting the trip back to the South Bronx. There was a beautiful little park beside a marina that seemed safe and quiet for sleeping. I spent the night there listening to the sound of the tide beating against the retaining wall. In the morning I walked to a nearby gas station to get a road map and chart the course home. The highway most appropriate for heading north seemed to be U.S. 1. Before leaving town I had to raise a little cash for the long trip ahead.

I presented myself as a donor at a blood bank in downtown Miami, lying about my age because the law prohibits donations by minors. The screening persons knew I was a minor but chose not to press the question. I was paid fifteen dollars for my blood. I now had the necessary enthusiasm to begin hitching north. The first ride came from a hippie driving an old beat-up Cadillac. He was on the way to Fort Lauderdale to spend the night in a shelter. He invited me to come along. I was feeling weak from minor withdrawal symptoms and it would make little sense to hitch at night, so I agreed to join him.

A religious organization ran the shelter in Fort Lauderdale. The residents were mostly winos and older white males who had dropped out of society. The crowded sleeping quarters consisted of bunk beds stacked as many as four high. The youngest person got to sleep on the top bunk. I was probably one of the few people there who could climb up to the top bunk without risking a fall. I saw right away that the residents were overly infantilized by the paid staff; these winos and social dropouts were treated as if they had never had another life. But I did not dwell for long on the inner workings of the shelter. My thoughts were mostly concerned with making it back to New York and my familiar Latino neighborhood: the sound of salsa music floating in the air, the stink of the old tenements, even the sight of my lousy junkie "friends."

The next day I was given a ride by a man pulling a mobile home with a Mercury. It was one of my most desperate afternoons on U.S. 1. I was feeling very tired and was consumed by the thought of being back home. The idea of hitching all the way to New York was losing its appeal. In desperation I tried to convince the man in the Mercury to lend me the money for a bus ticket to New

York. He told me a loan would not be possible. A river of tears poured from my eyes, but he was still not convinced of my need. Instead, he drove me to a local church in Cocoa Beach right beside the mall where the rest of his family was to meet him after shopping.

Full of hope, I knocked on the church door. The minister answered and led me into the study. I explained how I had come to Florida. I told him my mother had disowned me. It all started because my brother, Rudy, did not want to stay in junior high school; he decided to go to work at a local restaurant instead. Mother could not stand the idea of one of her sons dropping out of school; she demanded that Rudy either remain in school or move out. My brother was quite rebellious and determined to work; he left home. I protested to my mother about her ultimatum, claiming it unjust to expose a young child to homelessness. Mother would hear none of it. I was kicked out of the house too, for questioning her method of parenting. That was how I came to live on the streets.

The pastor listened to my story, but my cry seemed to fall on deaf ears. He said there was nothing he could do for me. He wished me luck in my attempt to reach New York and suggested I try another church in the next town.

I left the pastor's office very depressed. It surprised me that a Christian minister was unwilling to help a fourteen-year-old child. I walked back out to U.S. 1 and continued north toward the next major town, Daytona Beach. An old Chevy pulled up on the side of the road within a few minutes and the driver offered me a ride. The driver was a Black man on his way to a point just outside Daytona. I took comfort from the fact that we were both members of an oppressed class of people and shared a common experience of struggle. He drove around with a .22-caliber rifle carefully placed in the front seat of the car. "What's the rifle all about?" I asked.

"This twenty-two is for rednecks. This is the South, brother!" Racial tension was at an all-time high in 1969, the year I passed through Florida. I decided not to accept a ride from anyone even remotely resembling a redneck.

That was one way to avoid being found hanging from a
tree in the Florida marshlands.

Daytona Beach was humming with activity the day I
arrived. The auto racing season had started and tourists
were there from all around the country. A temporary
amusement park had been set up to cater to the recrea-
tional needs of visitors. The tourists gave me a perfect
opportunity to beg for money. In the face of every visitor
I could see a bus ticket to New York coming within my
grasp. I spent the night in a shelter located on the side of
town away from the tourist district. Shelters seem to be
geographically located at the edges of town, much as the
residents live spiritually at the margins of society.

The Daytona Beach winos were different from others I
had encountered. They seemed more curious about me.
What was a young kid doing in the shelter system? They
asked many other questions, particularly about my family.
"You have your whole life ahead of you, kid. Go home. Get
off the streets." I could only respond by telling them I had
not chosen the street life. We were all called out of restless
sleep and feverish nightmares at five thirty in the morning. We were given exactly half an hour to be in the mess
hall for morning prayers, coffee, and doughnuts. The residents of the shelter were expected to leave immediately
after breakfast. The Daytona winos would naturally return
in the evening to bunk down again. Their lives would
remain chained to the rituals surrounding shelter life. I did
not want to become a part of that dead culture.

I tried one more church in Daytona Beach but met a
very similar response. These Christians seemed to find it
easy to separate faith and love from those in need.

I went on to Jacksonville. While there I walked past a
restaurant, and a delicious food display attracted my attention. My eyes must have communicated my hunger because an elderly man sitting inside noticed me and invited
me to join him for dinner. He was quite shocked to hear
that I was traveling across Florida alone. A puzzled look
came over his face. I could almost hear the questions that
must have been running through his mind: Where are you

from? What are you doing in Florida by yourself? Where are your parents? Don't you know it could be dangerous hitching alone? He told me that he was a member of Alcoholics Anonymous and worked in the Florida prison system establishing AA groups. That evening there was a meeting in St. Augustine, which he planned to attend. I was invited to go along. I figured it would be an interesting way to spend a night. Meanwhile, in the back of my head, I was trying to find the words that would prompt him to lend me the money for a bus ticket to New York City.

The people attending the AA meeting were not the crowd I expected to find. Most were white professionals. For the first time I realized that addiction crosses all racial and class lines. It is certainly not the result of moral inferiority, as I had come to believe while in the ghetto. White people suffer the same problems. After the meeting, we went back to the old man's apartment, where he allowed me to spend the night on a sofa bed. The next morning he took me to the bus station, bought me a ticket to New York City, and promised to pray for me.

Back in New York City

I arrived in New York City on a cold winter night. The warm weather of Puerto Rico and Florida was still in my bones, but not for long. On the streets another side of me took over. The South Bronx was calling me. My body trembled, anticipating the fix to be enjoyed with Rudy and his friends. Heroin addiction is demon possession. The demon is an overwhelming compulsion to get high. I walked across Forty-second Street to the IRT #2 subway, which goes into the heart of the South Bronx. The Simpson Street station is the doorway to junkie paradise for Puerto Rican addicts. Rudy would be in the basement apartment waiting for an invitation to a fix. He was certainly going to be surprised to see me.

The South Bronx was supposed to be the place where my parents would realize the so-called American dream. When they arrived it was mostly Jewish, Irish, and Italian.

The steady growth of the Puerto Rican community caused a decline in the traditional South Bronx population. Mother dreamed that her children would have a slice of the American pie in the form of an education. My parents are simple folk, campesinos (peasants). They never had the option of formal education beyond the fourth grade. The promise of the good life never really came true, for them or for many other Latino immigrants in the neighborhood. Puerto Ricans were forced to worship in the basement of the local Catholic church, they worked in the factories for low pay, and their children were sent to the battlefront in Vietnam, or died under stairwells from drug overdoses, or were killed on the street. In my neighborhood, out of a group of fifteen decent kids, four have survived into their thirties. In 1985, Rudy himself would be found dead on the sidewalk.

Rudy was in the basement as I expected. Once he got over his anger, he was glad to see me. When someone disappears in the South Bronx, the person is probably either in jail or dead. I told Rudy all about my trips, to California, Puerto Rico, and Florida. Rudy sat through the narration of events simply shaking his head. People in the South Bronx hardly ever move to nicer neighborhoods. Junkies never move. For this reason Rudy was concerned about my disappearance. We often hear about those who disappear in El Salvador and Guatemala, but never the South Bronx. The National Guard is usually behind the disappearance of civilians in Central America. The campesinos have a very clear picture of their torturers. The poor of the South Bronx also know their executioners. In the barrio, people are killed on the streets by junkies, they die from drug overdoses, or they are apprehended by the immigration officer, La Migra.

I settled into a rhythm of shooting dope, hustling money on the streets, and doing all that was necessary to survive. I tried to deal dope in the neighborhood and was probably the youngest connection around. One afternoon, an old junkie couple cornered me in one of the area buildings. They claimed they wanted to buy dope, but their intentions were to rob me. The man went around behind me and held a carpet-cutting knife to my neck. As it was pressed against the jugular vein, the slightest move would have been fatal. The woman went through my pockets, removing the dope I had been given to sell. She wanted everything, but her boyfriend insisted she take only what was necessary to get "cured." I had thirty bags of dope in my pocket. The junkies left with twenty. Dealing dope was proving to be hazardous to one's health. I went to the supplier's house after the mugging to explain what had happened. I showed him the remaining ten bags. I could have told him the muggers took all the dope, but instead I told him the truth. Honest junkies have short lives on the streets of the South Bronx. I never returned to the connection after selling the last load of dope for him. Begging on the streets was more honest and far less dangerous. No way could I be a street mugger, dealer, second-story man, or shoplifter. I was destined to be the "Mister, can you spare a dime?" addict.

When I was fifteen, something happened that turned my life around. Two Presbyterian ministers who were active in the civil rights movement in Detroit and had marched with Dr. Martin Luther King, Jr., in the South came to New York City to engage in street ministry. The spirit of the civil rights movement was the driving force behind their commitment to reach persons for whom society had no safety nets. The gospel drove them into the streets in places like the South Bronx, the Lower East Side, and Harlem. These ministers decided to do more than merely talk about transforming the life of the poor and oppressed. They were attempting to model for the church a new form of transformative ministry. They were risking life and limb to join the struggle of the oppressed. They had marched in civil rights demonstrations and had bottles and rocks thrown at them by angry white racists. Now they pounded the streets of the South Bronx, entering filthy bars to talk with junkies and offer them help to recover. Most of the junkies in the neighborhood were impressed by their faith witness.

Ken Haines, one of these street ministers, made me a part of his own family. I had gone with him on a sightseeing trip to Washington, D.C. At the Lincoln Memorial we read Lincoln's moving Emancipation Proclamation while standing next to one of the majestic pillars that adorn the structure. We walked toward the reflecting pool and sat down under a tree. Ken said, "How would you like to come and live with my family, Hal?" I could not believe the offer. Ken was a white male Midwesterner, married, with three children—a Presbyterian minister at a peak in his career. Did he know what he was saying? His family and friends back in Ohio advised against the idea, as I later discovered. They believed one simply did not invite a fifteen-year-old Puerto Rican junkie to join the relatively peaceful home of a white middle-class family. It was not heard of in 1970.

There was some merit in these objections. The chances of a Puerto Rican junkie recovering and integrating into a new class and cultural setting were slight. But Ken had a deep sense of commitment and faith in the transforming dimensions of the gospel, which seemed to call him to a new form of ministry. I accepted the offer to live with his family and became the fourth child in the household. Ken's wife, Beth, treated me like one of her own sons. I found myself in the position of being an older brother to the Haineses' three children, Jeff, Ann, and Todd. The kids did not see me as a Puerto Rican or a junkie; instead I was Hal, their new older brother. I learned to overcome some of my distrust of white people, and they learned to see the humanity of Latinos. We learned to call one another mother, father, sister, brother, friend.

The Haines family was settling into a new home in New City, New York, at the time I went to live with them. I was placed in a twenty-one-day detoxification program run by Beth Israel Hospital's Bernstein Institute. The patients were mostly Black and Latino junkies from different parts of New York City. Many of them suffered the revolving-door syndrome. That is to say, they were regulars. Some had a history of drug use spanning eighteen years. They were familiar with every detox program in the Big Apple and had seen the inside of jail on many occasions. Their arms and hands were scarred and deformed.

During my first stay at Beth Israel I completed only nineteen of the required twenty-one days in the detox program. I wanted out. I walked into a drug counselor's office located on my hospital ward floor. The counselor's name was Marion, which to me seemed very strange. I had never met a man named Marion, so I presumed he was a wimp. "I am going to check out of the hospital—right now!" I yelled.

"You cannot check out without the signature of the admitting adult. I am not able to let you out unless they sign for you," was his reply.

My junkie side was taking control. "Look, if you don't let me out I'll destroy this office." I was prepared to hit him with a chair if necessary. Marion picked up the telephone and called the Haineses. Ken gave the necessary permission to have me discharged from the program. I left the hospital and went directly to the South Bronx to buy dope. Ken picked me up later that evening on Home Street.

The family was very disappointed with me. I was feeling a bit guilty about my actions too. They learned, however, that overcoming drug addiction is no easy task. A recovering junkie swings back and forth between an obsession with the drug and the desire to be addiction-free. I was sneaking into the city from time to time to get high. When Beth Haines discovered that I was doing this, she devised a plan that was supposed to embarrass me into staying clean. Basically, her plan consisted of piling the entire family into the car to take me into the city to buy dope. Beth believed I would not subject the whole family to such an experience. The plan did not work. I left the family in the car on a South Bronx street and went off to get high. Several weeks after this incident, I was taken back to Beth Israel and admitted into the detox program again.

My second stay at Beth Israel ended in much the same way. I just could not endure the full twenty-one days in the program. I pleaded with the Haineses over the telephone to come for me. I promised not to run off to the South Bronx and buy dope. Beth agreed, on condition that we return home immediately. The whole family showed up for me. It was summer, and we planned that I would enter high school in the fall. Ken was tutoring me in history and social studies. He also made theology a part of my study. His favorite theologians were Paul Tillich, Karl Barth, Reinhold Niebuhr, and Carl Michalson. I was encouraged to look through his library to find books to discuss with him. In the evenings I got into the routine of reading the kids to sleep. My first experience with children's stories came at this late point in my life. The family was giving me a great deal of support and love, yet I continued to sneak into the city from time to time. I finally had to confess to them. Together, we decided to try a methadone program as a way to facilitate my transition to a drug-free life.

Ken found a privately run methadone program managed by Gracie Square Hospital. I was usually given a one-week supply of methadone to take home. It is impossible to get high when you have methadone in your system. I gave up trying to shoot dope and started feeling good about myself for it. In August 1971, we went to the Rockland County School Board to find out how I could be enrolled in high school. There was a problem, however. The county regulations prohibited anyone not a legal guardian or custodian from enrolling a minor within the school system. We were given two alternatives: either the Haineses would obtain legal custody of me or my natural mother would sign a release. I was all for adoption because I already felt a part of the family, but I knew that my mother would never agree to give me up to a North American family. The Haineses were in for a mighty fascinating afternoon on the day we went to get her signature on the release form.

The whole family piled into the car one Sunday afternoon for the visit to my mother's apartment. I guided them up to apartment 3C, located in a tenement on Mapes Avenue, and knocked on the door. Mother answered and let us all in. I think the Haineses expected to find my mother living in filthy conditions; however, they saw a beautifully kept apartment. Mother escorted us to the living room, which was well furnished and clean. Beth explained that I was now living with them in New City, New York. I remember sitting in that living room, torn between two worlds. I wanted to return to my natural home, to my Puerto Rican roots, to the context of my Latino community, and to my mother's side. I loved the Haines family and was grateful to them, but their love could not replace the loss or fill the emptiness.

I asked my mother that afternoon to allow the Haineses to adopt me. "Over my dead body!" she yelled. Beth could not even convince her to sign the release form that would at least permit me to enroll in school. My mother would not allow me to come home, but she also refused to give me up. Fortunately, I was able to speak to her alone and get her to sign the form. The high value she placed on education would not allow her to turn her back on me completely.

Ken helped to develop my interest in liberation theology. During my high school years I spent a great deal of time reading books by Paul Tillich, Reinhold Niebuhr, Karl Barth, Frederick Herzog, James Cone, Erik Erikson, and Mark Twain. The other students seemed young in view of my own life experience, so I spent more time absorbed in books than in the schoolyard. Ken and I would have long discussions in the evenings about the social meaning of Christianity and the importance of loving effectively. Ken did not offer private explanations for faith; instead, he focused attention on the social or corporate aspects of the Christian life. His work in the civil rights struggle convinced him of the importance of incarnating faith in the form of acts of justice or realized love. One of Ken's favorite Christian philosophers was the Russian thinker Nicolas Berdyaev. Berdyaev's notion of personalism and his critique of the historical form of Marxism were topics of frequent conversation. Ken was a thoroughly existentialist pastoral theologian. At the College of Wooster, I went on to major in philosophy, writing my senior thesis on Berdyaev's major work, *Slavery and Freedom.*

Seminary

I was seriously debating going to seminary. Naturally, Ken was a very influential figure for me; however, I had developed a very strong interest in and love for critical philosophy. Part of me wanted to pursue graduate study in philosophy, but two of my college professors persuaded me to change my mind and attend seminary. First, one of my teachers nominated me for a Fund for Theological Education scholarship. Following an arduous selection process I was awarded a grant. Second, Professor James Haden, chairperson of the philosophy department and a former physicist turned Platonist, urged me to read Karl Jaspers' book on philosophical faith, entitled in English *The Perennial Scope of Philosophy.* Haden's suggestion masked the wealth of his wisdom. Karl Jaspers believed that the moment of greatest transcendence is revealed to human beings in "boundary situations." The moment of historical crisis reveals life's deepest meaning and authenticity. I suppose Haden was urging me to learn from my own experiences of alienation and crisis. He argued that I should attend seminary because I would be exposed to the traditions of both Western philosophical thought and theology. I chose to attend seminary but was still uncertain about going into ministry.

I was accepted by two seminaries: San Francisco Theological Seminary and Union Theological Seminary in New York City. I first leaned toward attending school on the West Coast but changed my mind while at Wooster. I enrolled at Union in the fall of 1978. It was time to return to New York City, time to get in touch with the multiple layers of my inner life, time to come to terms with my sense of historical crisis and discover authentic existence. I was feeling quite able to handle the city in which I was once a junkie living on the streets. I had become a fanatic of long-distance running in college, and my health was excellent.

My first year at Union was emotionally a disaster. I requested a leave of absence in the second semester. I needed time to think my life over. I felt alienated from the Puerto Rican population of the city, having moved for so many years in a white world. The students at Union Seminary were not the radicals I had imagined while I was back at Wooster. Most came from the Midwest and had predictable liberal viewpoints. Union Seminary's claim to be leading the way in urban theological education lacked substance. I was not sure where I fit into North American society. I was not white, and I was not Black, and my Latino identity was in a state of confusion. I went on leave and found a job with the financial newspaper *American Banker* with the glorified title of "research librarian."

Working at the newspaper gave me a look at the world of finance. The paper devoted itself to reporting, legitimating, defending, and idealizing the free market economy. Liberation theology was perceived by many on the staff as a threat to the financial stability of the West. The reporters misunderstood the goals of this theology. Liberation theologians have opted for the poor and, with the poor, are attempting to articulate a new direction for human life that is more just. The newspaper's position enabled me to understand the variety of forms in which idolatry can take hold of life. The reporters believed that profits constituted the fundamental reason for human existence. The emptiness and lovelessness of that posture gave me the insight I needed to open up to God's call to ministry. I returned to seminary the following fall with renewed motivation.

I had started my second year of seminary education but was still not convinced I should enter the ordained ministry. My experience at the newspaper had caused me to return to seminary, yet I was reluctant to translate that experience into a decision to enter the ministry and dedicate my life to the struggle for right relationships. The church did not appear to be on the cutting edge of social justice issues. True, the church exercised an important symbolic role in the life of society, but its moral positions too often failed to lead to concrete action on behalf of the oppressed. Street life taught me that all talk is cheap. The church did not appear to be the new community it had been called to be, but rather part of the problem.

My aversion to organized religion diminished under the influence of another Presbyterian minister, the Rev. Charles T. Yerkes, who was doing doctoral work at Union. Chuck Yerkes was in his late forties when we met. Years earlier he had graduated from Princeton Theological Seminary's Master of Divinity program. He was ordained in 1962. Starting out in a local parish in New York City, Chuck was drawn into more specialized forms of ministry and dedicated his life to serving the voiceless of North American society. He worked with street gangs, with militant young adults, and in New York City's criminal justice system. Because Chuck is a white male he could have lived a privileged life; instead, he chose to do ministry in places like the Lower East Side, helping the oppressed poor understand their own power to transform life. Chuck attempted to love effectively wherever he could invest himself. His witness reinforced my experience with the Haines family.

My last year of seminary found me still undecided regarding the future and ordination. Union Seminary's student body was becoming active around the South African apartheid issue and calling for the seminary to divest. I was glad to see a wave of ethical action overtaking the student body. The seminary did not respond to the challenge in the spirit of the gospel. The trustees and administration chose to side with the status quo. On another occasion, the seminary support staff was unionizing itself and the seminary administration did everything possible to undermine the process. I was confused by Union's hypocrisy and lack of faithful witness to the concerns of justice for the least among us.

During this period of time I entered a special program that involved integrating theological education with service in the parish. I was selected to be a student pastor at a local United Methodist church, Broadway Temple–Spanish. I was to serve the Spanish-speaking charge of the church.

My year as a student pastor brought me to a definite decision to enter the ordained ministry. The congregation nurtured a strong biblical faith within me. I learned to do theology in the context of a community fighting the assaults of racism and economic oppression. The members of the Spanish-speaking congregation were very much oriented to private faith; however, the biblical themes of liberation and promise still had social dimensions for most of them. Biblical faith came to mean for me a political commitment to the liberation of the oppressed.

I became a member of Broadway Temple–Spanish, a congregation that was then under the leadership of the Rev. Noé Torres. The tension between Latin American liberation theology and Latino evangelical piety developed as a major theme of my faith perceptions. Generally, it is assumed that evangelical faith is conservative and reactionary, especially around issues of left-oriented social action. Many traditional Latino church groups in the United States would fit the conservative description because they have tended not to be influenced by the sweeping theological changes initiated by the Latin American bishops' conferences of the last two decades. Until very recently, the North American Latino church has led an isolated life cut off from the new theology coming out of the Third World. As a student pastor at Broadway Temple–Spanish, I was convinced that the Latino evangelical in the United States, or any evangelical, could recover the social-witness dimensions latent in the pietistic tradition.

Evangelical faith has its roots in seventeenth-century German pietism. Paul Tillich believed that German pietism made two great contributions to the Christian faith. First, it gave the church missionary zeal. Second, it called people to work for justice on behalf of the poor and oppressed.[1] These dimensions of evangelical faith seemed important to recover from the past. When I became pastor of the Church of All Nations, I was given the opportunity to lead the worshiping community in this quest for the integration of private faith and social witness.

BEEN WAITING

*Rudy's waiting on the corner for his
big hit. he's been waiting now for
ten years and the tracks in his arms
where Señora Heroina does come quiets*

*him for the wait while promising a
more complete destiny someday. he's
been waiting for the lover he
dreams of, for bitterness to run away,*

*for a blade of grass to grow from the
crack in the sidewalk that he stares
at in the wait, for Orchard Beach*

*to be in his pocket so he can reach in
for a calm feel to living; he's been waiting
for the welfare check, for the roaches to
take a walk from his one room where there*

*ain't no food no way. he's been waiting to
kick a jones* he doesn't have, for his mother
who long ago said good-bye, for his country to*

*be born in him. he's been waiting for Lelo, who
left the waiting corner to join the navy and kick
his brothers' asses down in Vieques under orders*

*just to live. he's been waiting for spring and
summer and fall and forget about winter because
the corner is cold. he's been waiting for the*

*right time of day or night to think about
waiting some more.*

---

*habit

2

Hear This Cry

The face of poverty could be seen everywhere that evening, as some church members and I walked through the Puerto Rican barrio of the Lower East Side of Manhattan. We were on our way to hold a home prayer service for a shut-in. One cannot walk through el barrio without seeing dilapidated tenements, empty lots piled high with rotting garbage, winos who have passed out on the sidewalks, junkies dealing on the street corners, and homeless families gathered on the front steps of abandoned buildings. A stench of decay fills the air. As we walked, one of the women commented, "When I first moved into this neighborhood in 1948 it was not like this. It was clean and safe. I remember it was mostly Jewish, Italian, and Polish. Now, it's a Puerto Rican barrio. We just don't know how to take care of things. I can't understand it. We didn't live like this on the island."

Josefa's comments went to the very heart of the question of the existence of ghettos and barrios. Who or what is responsible for the conditions of life in which the poor live on the Lower East Side? Where do the poor come from? Are Puerto Ricans unable to take care of their neighborhood? Are they morally inferior and thus destined to live in wretchedness? Josefa's explanation for the situation of the Puerto Rican poor in the barrio was based on a subjective judgment: that Puerto Ricans are morally irresponsible and therefore their character deficiency causes social decay, which leads to the existence of ghettos. Josefa blamed the Puerto Ricans for their poverty,

unemployment, low educational achievement, homelessness, drug abuse, poor health, and deplorable living conditions.

Josefa's understanding of what causes poverty reflected
the perception that is dominant in U.S. society. On one
occasion I was invited to preach in a small town in West
Virginia. Many of the members of the church were in
positions of leadership and influence in the town. I shared
with the congregation a number of images of the South
Bronx and the Lower East Side. After the service, people
expressed a sense of moral outrage at the situation in
which the Puerto Rican poor are living. Most were very
sympathetic, but they could not break out of the individ-
ual-focused explanation for the existence of the barrio.
One person vigorously shook my hand, saying, "Why do
people live that way? They should relocate to another
community that offers better work opportunities and living conditions." Naturally, this suggestion makes a great
deal of sense—even to the poor in el barrio. The reality
causing the wretchedness of the poor in the barrio is seldom uncovered by commonsense analysis. Josefa and
some of the persons I talked with after the service at the
church in West Virginia began their analysis on a false
premise—that the individual causes his or her own poverty and oppression. The commonsense explanation tends
to blame the individual by suggesting that he or she lives
in subhuman conditions as a matter of choice.

The Puerto Rican poor are hardworking people. Yet no
matter how hard they work, there is little improvement in
their life chances as a result. José came to the United States
from Puerto Rico in 1952. The farm economy of Puerto
Rico, upon which he depended for a living, had by then
been ruined by North American agribusiness. José was a
sugarcane farmer for whom an industrializing economy
meant hardship and unemployment. He could not make
a living at farming, and the industrializing economy had
fewer jobs than workers. Thus he had to come to the
United States in search of work. José found a job in the
light manufacturing industry that fueled New York's econ-

omy in the 1950s and took up residence in the Lower East Side of Manhattan—known to the Puerto Rican community as "Loisaida." His wife and five children joined him in New York five months later.

José believes it is a man's duty to take care of his family. A friend once suggested he go on welfare to help support the family during a period of economic crisis which he was experiencing. José refused, saying, "My children are not the mayor's children! I will provide for them by the fruits of my own labor." José was a man of deep principles and traditional values. The notion of public assistance was not in itself offensive; he believed the government was obligated to care for its citizens. However, welfare was not for him. Eventually his work-ethic philosophy of life enabled him to save enough money to buy a bodega, a grocery store. But he extended credit to so many people who needed it that he was not able to pay the bills, and he lost the store. Hard work did not make a rich man out of José. He lived out his last years in a low-income public housing project and suffered from ill health. Racial discrimination, economic marginalization, and the language barrier combined to keep him for a lifetime in the ranks of the Puerto Rican poor.

It is not surprising that Josefa's perceptions about the barrio and poverty were similar to those of members of the West Virginia church. National life is characterized by a certain uniformity in the way people think and feel. We think, feel, and desire almost exactly the same things. Our political and economic institutions determine our thoughts about the world that surrounds us, providing the substance of our conventional judgments. In the end, the uniformity of our perceptions places us at the service of the status quo.[1] In the process we learn to serve our neighbor in the spirit of indifference.

Life is ordered by forces outside us. Big corporations control the national economy and create advertising campaigns to appeal to the national soul in the spirit of consumerism. The domestic economy is currently connected to a global system of militarism and monetary schemes

The jingles of consumerism have emerged as the hymns of the age. Our thoughts are no longer fully our own; indeed, the vast majority of people have lost the capacity to be critical of the system.[2] Many seem to believe it is un-American to demand that human life be given a higher priority than the concern for profits.

President Reagan's administration elevated George Orwell's "newspeak" to the level of art; for example, it claimed that Central Americans fleeing political persecution are merely economic refugees; Nicaragua is a communist and terrorist regime; the Iran-contra affair did not violate the Constitution of the United States because the illegal arms trading with Iran was done both to free the Middle East hostages and to provide funds for Nicaraguan "freedom fighters"; U.S. citizens go hungry and are homeless or unemployed as a matter of personal choice; the elderly are not suffering economic hardship; and only a large military budget can assure global peace. The acceptance of the official picture of reality diminishes one's capacity to judge reality. Influenced by such newspeak, the majority of people have surrendered willingly to false needs and perceptions.

Without some critical awareness of how their lives are modified and transformed by the controlling myths of the ruling forces in society, persons are reduced to functions in a large machine. The role of the individual soon becomes that of adjusting to society. For instance, the Statue of Liberty celebrations held in 1986 represent a clear example of the public's uncritical acceptance of the official picture of reality. People all around the country fixed their gaze on the beautiful "mother of exiles" symbolizing compassion and justice the world over. But the mass media concentrated their reports on issues that had an entertainment value. President Reagan celebrated the occasion from the aircraft carrier *John F. Kennedy,* which only weeks before had launched an attack on Libya based on false intelligence reports. President Pinochet of Chile was allowed to sail his torture ship, the *Esmeralda,* as part of the liberty celebration. While we focused on the Statue

of Liberty celebration in Hollywood style, persons searching for safe haven in the United States were being turned
away; the Reagan administration was supporting the
South African white government by increasing the sale of
military armaments to it; money was being raised for the
contras by whatever means necessary; and the civil wars
in El Salvador and Guatemala were escalating because of
U.S. support for brutal regimes. What was really being
celebrated on July 4, 1986? Was it the values of compassion and justice? Or did we actually celebrate the surrender of freedom and critical judgment?

Storefront Latino churches on the Lower East Side of
Manhattan promote in their members a noncritical relationship to society; indeed, the basic message of the Latino
fundamentalist church is one of social adjustment and assimilation into the system. First, the gospel is transformed
into a message of survival. The "sanctified" members are
armed with a language and a worldview that enable them
to deal with the chaos of the urban barrio. Second, the
Christian ethic is transformed into the command to sup-
press one's libido. The resounding challenge of the gospel
to the current order of social life is replaced by the gospel
of self-control. These churches' theological worldview
supports the dominant social myths that stand behind the
loss of the capacity to exercise critical judgment.

I had an opportunity to work closely with a group of
seventy-two families who were homesteading over a period of ten years in three tenements. The families represented a rainbow collection of people: Puerto Rican,
Black, Asian, undocumented aliens, and poor whites. The
City of New York actually owned the buildings occupied
by the families, but they were allowed to live in them with
the understanding that eventually the residents would be
accepted into an official "homesteading" program leading
to ownership of the tenements. In 1981 the city agency
that manages municipal property, the Department of
Housing Preservation and Development (HPD), started
eviction proceedings against all of the families. The Lower
East Side was being gentrified with the help of HPD.

Storefront fundamentalist Latino churches typically side with the city government on housing issues. On one occasion, members of a storefront church attended community board meetings to voice opposition to homesteaders living in an abandoned tenement next to their church hall; the pastor argued that the homesteaders had no respect for the law. Members of such churches do not recognize homesteading as a movement that challenges the housing-for-profit system.

The Church of All Nations was approached by the homesteaders, who came one Sunday asking for our support. We helped them find legal representation and organized a housing coalition with them. (More will be said about this in chapter 4.) HPD argued that it was moving the families out of the three buildings for their own protection. Representatives of the HPD claimed the buildings were not habitable; moreover, they asserted that the city has a responsibility to house persons in shelters before aiding homesteading families. HPD completely forgot about the promises it made to the seventy-two families regarding their right to live in the buildings.

The real issue being debated in the case of the homesteaders versus HPD concerned the nature of real estate speculation. Because so many persons in the community lacked the capacity to judge the situation critically, it appeared that the homesteaders were preventing the development of housing for the poor. In fact, HPD was being used to serve the interests of private real estate firms seeking to buy city-owned buildings on the Lower East Side of Manhattan, which has become a haven for young urban professionals. The buildings occupied by the seventy-two families were designated to be sold to the highest-bidding private developer. Thus a public institution was being used to secure the private gain of a wealthy class with no interest in the housing needs of low-income and poor families. Ironically, the former commissioner of HPD resigned public office to take a job with a premier real estate developer. Fortunately, the homesteaders' case was upheld by the court.

Sociological Reflection on the Barrio Poor

More than two million Puerto Ricans live in the United States. The Puerto Rican community is a very youthful one, with a median age of 20.7 years.[3] Consequently, it has been hit hard by the domestic budget cuts between 1978 and 1987 in the areas of education, housing, health care, and employment training programs. Mike and Delia once lived in a three-room apartment while employed in a job training program underwritten by the Comprehensive Employment and Training Act of 1973 (CETA). President Reagan's administration dismantled CETA and thereby caused many people like Mike and Delia to lose their homes and an opportunity to improve their chances in life. The couple currently lives in one of the Lower East Side's shantytown communities. Mike and Delia have built a home for themselves out of discarded plywood and other materials they were able to collect around the neighborhood. A Puerto Rican flag is blown by barrio breezes to and fro just outside the doorway that leads into their little shack. Across the street from that shantytown is a construction site where a new housing complex is being built, but their financial situation will not allow them to apply for an apartment.

I talked with Mike and Delia one afternoon during a visit to the shantytown community. Mike said, "Puerto Ricans are victims of North American apartheid. We don't mean a damn thing to whites! Look how they took control of our island. We are not human beings to them. We are simply animals who work to make them rich. We are the people who push the coat racks down Seventh Avenue and clean the toilets in the fancy buildings on Wall Street, the people they don't want to sit next to on the subway. They should come and eat at my table to know who we are. All you have to do is look around this community. The kids are dropping out of school left and right, crack is taking over their lives, and gentrification is pushing us to the margins. Puerto Ricans are the new Invisible Man!"

In our value system the choice between success and

failure is considered to be the responsibility of the individual. Community and individual problems are not understood in terms of social and structural realities. Puerto Rican marginalization is blamed on the individual rather than on larger systemic problems. Many persons would argue that Mike and Delia have failed as individuals to take advantage of society's opportunities for advancement. The couple has simply not kept up with the system. Public policy and racial discrimination are not seen as factors contributing to Mike and Delia's impoverishment; indeed, shantytowns are simply places where the lazy and good-for-nothing members of society go to drop out. Social barriers have nothing to do with failure to get ahead. We constantly venerate the individual, even to the extent of believing that the affluence and global influence of the United States are the result of the accomplishments of certain individuals. Individuals of "low achievement" are never worth veneration. Who cares about a shantytown community?

What are some of the causes of poverty and Puerto Rican marginalization within the dominant society? Can we attribute the low social and economic status of Puerto Ricans to inferior moral development? The myth of individualism has taught most of us to believe that marginalization and poverty are signs of personal failure or moral deficiency. Traditionally it is believed that society is full of opportunities for the hardworking individual. Social mobility is made possible in our society because it operates out of a system of "fair play."

William Ryan wrote a book entitled *Equality*,[4] in which he proposes two categories through which to examine competition in our society. First, Ryan examines the "fair play" category. This category is the most dominant in the United States. Fair players believe that America is a land of equal opportunity for all. According to fair players, individuals are rewarded by society on the basis of merit. Fair players characteristically support the free enterprise system and identify strongly with the social myths that focus on the centrality of the individual in life's struggles.

Fair players are convinced that social inequality in the
United States results from private problems. In other
words, racial discrimination, economic exploitation, and
the nature of the distribution of wealth in North American
society have nothing to do with the structure of inequality.
Second, Ryan talks a little about the "fair shares" category.
Basically, people in this group tend to believe that all
persons have a right to share equally in the resources of
society. Fair sharers see social inequality in terms of social
and structural issues. They are a minority group in U.S.
society. They tend not to subscribe to the myth of the
individual but look to systemic factors to explain social
reality.

Why do so many Puerto Ricans affirm the "fair play"
perspective? My mother has been a hardworking woman
all her life. She believes in this perspective. All her life she
has believed that hard work would improve her social
status, but she has lived on minimum wages since she
began working in her teens. I remember Mother going to
work in the garment district from 9 A.M. to 6 P.M. each day
of the week while trying to raise my brother and sister and
me in a two-room apartment. At night we all helped her
do a second job, which involved sitting around the kitchen
table making costume jewelry. I can still smell the glue.
Remarkably, Mother found time to attend beauty school
and obtain a barber's license. Yet, by and large, her pursuit
of the American dream brought very little real change to
her difficult life. "Fair play" has not returned all it promised to that hardworking woman who dreamed of making
it in the United States.

Racial discrimination has had a part in shaping the social
world of the Puerto Rican. I was fifteen years old before
I came to the realization that Puerto Ricans are not all
junkies, thieves, prostitutes, or pimps. The prevailing negative sociological images of Puerto Ricans were accepted
even by the Puerto Rican community. The racism of the
dominant society functioned to promote negative images
of Latinos, which in turn had lasting effects in the barrio.
The impact of the sociology of racism can be seen in the

despair of the younger generation. Eight out of every ten
Puerto Rican youths drop out of high school. On Manhattan's Lower East Side, these kids can be found in the park
beside the East River. A highway runs alongside the park
carrying suburbanites to and from work in the city. Puerto
Rican youths hanging around the park are just so many
faces seen from the cars that pass by. The suburbanites will
never hear about the time Lelo overdosed beneath the
Manhattan Bridge, or the time Rosa was raped at the far
end of the park, or the day Pee Wee was stabbed to death
over a twenty-dollar bag of dope.

All Puerto Rican youths do not drop out of school because they lack motivation or an "adequate family structure." These may be attributable causes in certain cases;
however, more complicated factors are at work. First, the
general indifference of U.S. society toward the Puerto
Rican community must be seen as one factor with a negative impact on young people. Second, the lack of bilingual
and bicultural educational programs encourages Latino
youths to drop out. Third, the use of IQ tests—tests that
measure the middle-class ethos—contributes to the mis-
placement of Latino youths in the classroom.[5] I have a
friend who was put in a class for the seriously retarded
because he failed an IQ test, although he did not know any
English at the time. The problem was eventually corrected, and today he is a lawyer. But his case is an excep-
tion. In many instances, the problem is never corrected
and children are damaged for life.

Poor housing conditions are a part of the wretched social reality of the Puerto Rican family. The South Bronx,
the Lower East Side, and East Harlem are symbols of
government abandonment. The list of presidential candi-
dates who campaigned in the South Bronx alone reads like
a Who's Who of American political life. Yet even when
they were elected, nothing changed for the people of the
South Bronx. In 1987, 61 percent of the population of the
South Bronx never finished high school; about 40 percent
of the households had to live on welfare; some 32.6 percent of the families had an annual income below $5,000;

and 59.2 percent of the families made less than $10,000 a year.[6]

The myth of the individual on which the social philosophy of the United States is based has been incarnated as social Darwinism. The concept of "fair play" has reinforced the vicious cycle of Puerto Rican social alienation and marginalization. The game enables the haves to feed themselves on the system, while the have-nots are sent away with nothing but the fictitious American dream. And many of those who suffer most under the current social reality have been successfully enlisted to defend the individual-centered system.

Political Marginalization: A View from the Barrio

In 1898, the Spanish colony of Puerto Rico became the possession of the United States. The Treaty of Paris, signed that year, gave the United States control of the island, including the right to determine its political fate. The flag of the United States of America was flown from all public buildings on the island, marking the start of the new colonial rule. Indeed, a people with a different language and culture would now exercise colonial power.[7] Once the eagle landed on Puerto Rican soil, the island's political institutions began to be transformed to promote North American norms and interests to the detriment of the inhabitants. The marginalization of Puerto Ricans from the centers of power has been the legacy of San Juan Hill. In 1900, Congress passed the Foraker Act, giving the United States total control over the political-administrative affairs of the island and completing the marginalization of the political power of the local landlords.[8]

From 1898 to 1940 the island of Puerto Rico was transformed into a captive market for U.S. goods. The colonial government served North American interests, making Puerto Rico an investment backyard for U.S. capital. The American dollar was in full possession of the island's economy during these four decades; indeed, the colonial government, empowered by legislative acts of Congress, facilitated the downward mobility of Puerto Ricans. The Puerto Rican people have never fully recovered from the experience; indeed, the reality of political marginalization on the island continues to find expression in the urban centers to which they migrated in the States.[9]

The Protestant Church played a major role in the development of the colonial reality. It secured a place for North America in the hearts and minds of Puerto Ricans by invoking the name of God. Puerto Ricans learned to pray in English, and to pledge allegiance to the United States flag, because of the evangelizing efforts of Protestant missionaries,[10] many of whom believed that divine providence had guided the United States to the island in order to elevate the people to the highest standards of Christian civilization.

The Protestant Church's religious effort was clearly associated with the colonial project. The United States was understood as the earthly manifestation of the heavenly kingdom, instrument of salvation for the world. Many Protestant missionaries believed that the United States was solely responsible for having raised the banners of civilization and salvation over the hills of San Juan. In fact, most Puerto Ricans see these banners as less than noble. The colonial reality has meant economic exploitation and oppression. Puerto Ricans have fought in U.S.-sponsored wars, have been cruelly exploited by North American corporate investors, and have been condemned to life in the barrio. The systematic process of marginalization of political life, whose foundation was laid in the first four decades of U.S. rule, has hardly reflected the virtues of civilization and salvation.

Colonial rule in Puerto Rico caused an immediate transformation of the governing institutions of society, including church and state. Protestant missionaries built schools through which to carry out the colonial plan of ideologically converting Puerto Ricans to the ethos of North American society; indeed, a major attempt was under way between 1898 and 1940 to "denationalize" the Puerto Rican consciousness. The cultural assimilation of any colony is a first sign of the destruction of national identity in the colonized.[11] The colonial project has sought to assimilate Puerto Ricans into North American white society. The white cultural assault has been facilitated by the colonial political machinery set up in Puerto Rico. This dates back to the passage of the Foraker Act of 1900, which established a system of public education designed to promote the Americanization of islanders, in addition to displacing Puerto Ricans from positions of decision making in government. Assimilation into white society has been expected of Puerto Ricans both on the island and in the United States. Yet, by and large, the racist structure of white society has kept Puerto Ricans marginal even when they wished to assimilate.

The generation that emigrated to the United States in the late 1940s and early 1950s fully experienced the cultural assault of white society. However, that generation held a fairly positive attitude toward the United States because of the success of the colonial government and the Protestant Church's ideological conversion project. Protestant missionaries made Christianity synonymous with the North American system of free enterprise. An old Puerto Rican domino player described the political and cultural dilemma experienced by Puerto Ricans when he said, "I am an American. Puerto Rico should stay the way it is—a commonwealth! That's best for it. Look, we have cars, food stamps, housing projects, citizenship, and all that. How many Latin American countries have this! If some of these other Latin American countries had what we have, they'd choose commonwealth too. It's a blessing. That's what it is, all right!" Charley is a real defender of United States colonialism, although he is a victim. He was forced out of his work as a sugarcane cutter in Puerto Rico and now works at minimum wage as a sheet-metal cutter in a factory in the South Bronx.

Pedro Albizu Campos (1891–1965), who headed the Nationalist movement in Puerto Rico, mounted a vigorous counterattack on the denationalization project. Albizu had studied in the United States at both the University of

Vermont and Harvard University. He received a law degree in 1923 from Harvard. In law school, Albizu developed a strong interest in international relations and
liberation movements around the world.[12] He dedicated
himself to the struggle for Puerto Rico's independence as
the only way to prevent the denationalization of Puerto
Ricans. Most islanders did not respond to Albizu's revolutionary cry; indeed, he was a lone prophet in the wilderness of colonial society. But in the 1960s, Pedro Albizu
Campos emerged as a symbolic figure for Puerto Ricans in
barrios in the United States who participated in the civil
rights movement.[13]

Puerto Rican political marginalization on the island continued to be a significant part of Puerto Rican experience
in the United States. However, the church did emerge in
the context of the barrio as a political institution that bore
both the culture and the political dreams of the community. Because people of Irish and Italian descent were
predominant in the Roman Catholic Church, Puerto Ricans found the Pentecostal tradition more open to them.
The Pentecostal church became one of the first institutions in U.S. society that enabled Puerto Ricans to exercise
some semblance of political power.[14] Despite its limita-
tions, that church played a decisive role in nurturing the
political aspirations of the Puerto Rican poor. It also contributed to the dismantling of marginalizing barriers
erected by white society. The negative images that white
society projected of Puerto Ricans were dispelled by the
Pentecostal church's positive ones. The Pentecostal
church has brought about great personal change.

Mario was one of the most feared muggers in the South
Bronx. His heroin habit cost $100 a day to support. Thus
he often preyed on people in the neighborhood, although
suburban junkies were his favorite victims. He would offer
to buy dope for them and simply then give them a bag of
baby powder. If they attempted to challenge him, Mario
didn't think twice before sticking them with his knife. He
was not the kind of person one would expect to have a
conversion experience that would change his life. Yet this

is exactly what did happen. Some street preacher happened to touch him in such a way that he gave up being a junkie and mugger.

After his personal conversion experience Mario entered a detoxification program and began attending a local storefront Pentecostal church. Soon he was back on the streets, with a Bible underneath his arm instead of a knife in his pocket. The neighborhood junkies did not take him seriously. They were sure he would go back on dope. However, Mario continued to preach to the junkies in the neighborhood, and he made sure no one sold drugs to the students at the local junior high school. Mario talked to these kids about drugs and even organized a community-based antidrug campaign. The most hated junkie in the neighborhood had changed into a friend of the people.

The Pentecostal church is capable of mobilizing people. Mario can certainly bear witness to this fact. Yet the political sensibilities of that church are not always the most progressive and helpful to the Puerto Rican poor. In fact, by tending to promote the political and religious views of the Protestant missionary church of Puerto Rico, the Pentecostal church has often contributed to the political marginalization of the Puerto Ricans in the barrio. The Pentecostal church has encouraged Puerto Ricans to perceive the United States as a defender of Christian civilization. Regrettably, this traditional defense of the political status quo has not helped to advance the deeper yearnings of Puerto Ricans for participation in the institutions that govern life. Yet the positive contributions of the Pentecostal church to the life of the Puerto Rican poor must be taken seriously.

By and large, Puerto Rican Protestants and Catholics have aligned themselves with the liberal political establishment. The political options considered by the Latino community in the United States have centered on the question of separation or integration. Political debates in the barrio have argued over the virtues of separating from white society at the cultural level while integrating at the economic level. Separatists believe that one way to over-

come the political marginalization of the Puerto Rican in
white society is to establish counterinstitutions for the purpose of developing the economic, political, religious, and
cultural areas of Latino life. Integrationists believe that
only by exercising the full rights of citizenship within
white society can political marginalization be supplanted.
North American society has been exposed to this debate
by the Black community through such thinkers as Booker
T. Washington and W. E. B. Du Bois, Martin Luther King,
Jr., and Malcolm X. Clearly, the debate indicates how social problems within oppressed communities in the
United States are perceived in terms of integration or
separation from a given political structure. Alternative
models for the administration of society are seldom projected by either the Black or the Puerto Rican community.

The current political establishment has not been successfully democratized by Puerto Ricans or by other oppressed
communities of color. In New York City, Puerto Ricans are
grossly underrepresented in government. The news media
pay little attention to the positive achievements of the
handful of legitimate Latino politicians, while they are
quick to point the finger at those who make a living by
pocketing money from programs for the poor. These factors combine to ensure that Puerto Ricans continue to
remain marginal to political life in the United States.

Puerto Ricans born in the United States in the early
1950s were radicalized during the '60s and '70s. This generation grew up in one of the most turbulent periods of the
nation's history, so it tends to be far more militant than any
other. This militant generation is characterized by its political radicality, economic improvement, internalization
of consumer values, and alienation from the church. Many
Puerto Ricans born in the United States in the 1950s feel
more at ease speaking English. This generation of Puerto
Ricans has tended to believe that the Spanish-speaking
church has not helped Latinos overcome their political
marginalization in U.S. society.

Third World liberation movements were on the rise
during the 1960s and 1970s. Puerto Ricans growing up in

the barrio saw these movements as successful challenges to white society. During the civil rights movement, Puerto Ricans in the barrio discovered their inner beauty and power along with the Blacks. Puerto Ricans marched under the motto of "Boricua power." (Boricua is derived from Borinquén, the name used by the Indians of the pre-Columbian period to refer to the island of Puerto Rico.) The nationalism developing in the Puerto Rican community at the time was given expression in such organizations as the Young Lords, the Puerto Rican Student Union, the Puerto Rican Socialist Party, and the Committee for the Independence of Puerto Rico.

The Young Lords embodied a New Left barrio strategy for overcoming political marginalization. They organized sympathetic Puerto Ricans in the barrio around clear issues: Puerto Ricans were in the United States because of negative economic shifts on the island; they suffered racist discrimination in the United States; they were an exploited class under capitalism; radical socialism was the only true political alternative; and the independence of Puerto Rico must be unconditional.[15] The category of liberation was central to the Young Lords' political strategy for overcoming marginalization. In a sense, this more radical element opened the way for moderate and liberal Puerto Rican and Latino politicians to gain acceptance in the political landscape of U.S. white society.

Economic Issues

Puerto Ricans were systematically dispossessed of their land by the colonial government set up by the United States. Brigadier General Guy V. Henry, who served as the first military governor in Puerto Rico, governed the island's affairs in a tactless and strong-handed manner. Henry did not respect the freedom of the press, especially when it was critical of the so-called reform program he implemented: an economic restructuring project that called for the freezing of all forms of credit, devaluation of the peso, and land-price fixing.[16]

Puerto Rican landowners were devastated by Henry's economic program. Many had to liquidate their holdings under pressure from North American capital interests. Puerto Ricans were increasingly left jobless and impoverished. Agriculture was diversified prior to the U.S. occupation, but investors now introduced monocultivation of the land, transforming Puerto Rico into one big sugar plantation.

Absentee sugar investors gradually forced islanders from the farms. Puerto Ricans had to find ways to sell their labor. In the early 1900s they emigrated to places like Hawaii and St. Croix to find work because of the high rate of unemployment in their native land. They managed to locate seasonal jobs, but there was very little social advancement to be found in the process. For instance, jobs in Hawaii's sugarcane fields were very limited. The excess supply of labor meant that wages were very low. Puerto Ricans merely found themselves pushed into deeper impoverishment and exploitation in the Polynesian cane fields.[17]

From 1898 to 1940, U.S. capital took over Puerto Rico's economy, causing a reshaping of the island's labor force and economic structure. Puerto Rico became a captive market. Salaries decreased and imported consumer goods increased; foreign capital exploited the island's resources; the military occupied large portions of the island; monoculture farming came into practice; and the system of government was tied to the United States.[18] In other words, all the signs of colonialism could be discerned in Puerto Rican society. Negative forces operating during these four decades secured the economic marginalization and downward mobility of Puerto Ricans. The profit reaped by U.S. capitalists from sugar plantations was made possible by banishing Puerto Ricans to certain pauperism.

The coffee industry was left to decline, because tariff regulations made sugar more profitable. The coffee-producing regions of the island saw a sharp decrease in work opportunities that forced farmers to move to the sugar-producing areas of the island. The coastal cane-growing areas and the adjacent urban centers experienced huge population increases. This gave hungry and unemployed Puerto Rican farmers little room for hope. By 1935, Puerto Rican agriculture was in a state of decline. Social stress increased because of the failed economy. Yet overpopulation was blamed as the chief cause of Puerto Rican hardship and economic depression.[19] The colonial economic structure was never identified as the source of the problem.

By 1940, industrialization was hailed as the solution to Puerto Rico's economic problems. Operation Bootstrap was introduced as the premier plan for economic salvation. In fact, Operation Bootstrap saved North American capital, but it condemned Puerto Ricans to even worse levels of economic marginalization. The plan encouraged them to migrate to the United States, it gave huge tax breaks to U.S. businesses, and it assured a cheap labor pool. Puerto Rico became one big factory. Operation Bootstrap never created the surplus jobs it promised. Between 1948 and 1965, Puerto Rico's colonial economy was revitalized but the work force decreased, as did employment opportunities.[20] The failure of Operation Bootstrap to meet the needs of Puerto Ricans sparked a massive migration of islanders to urban and agricultural centers in the United States; indeed, one third of the population of Puerto Rico headed to the States to find work.[21]

Puerto Ricans in the United States helped to create the high profits of the agricultural and textile industries. For instance, the garment industry sells more than $7 billion in clothing each year. New York City's garment industry accounts for about 70 percent of the country's wholesale garment trade. Puerto Rican labor has kept most of the textile industry in New York and made it competitive with manufacturers overseas.[22] In many respects, Puerto Ricans have served as a convenient Third World labor force inside of the United States.

Puerto Ricans have worked as migrant farmers in the United States since the 1950s. Agricultural interests in the 1930s managed to block the extension of employee protection laws to farm workers. The National Labor Relations Act of 1935, which established the right to form unions and practice collective bargaining, excludes migrant farmers. The Fair Labor Relations Act (1938), which set minimum wages and established the length of the standard workweek, also excluded migrant farmers from protection. Thus, Puerto Rican migrant farmers are by law left to suffer unimaginable social and economic hardship. Puerto Rican migrant farmers receive no overtime pay, workmen's compensation, or unemployment insurance. They live in substandard housing and are given poor health care; their children receive extremely poor educations.[23]

Puerto Rican migrant farmers are recruited to harvest crops in New Jersey every year. They live and work in conditions resembling slavery. Often, eight or more persons live in a single room designed for no more than three. The lack of laundry services means that dirty sheets are used to cover torn mattresses. Puerto Rican migrant farmers on many of the farms in New Jersey are not allowed to receive visitors. Farm camps are often as far as ten miles from the nearest town, which means migrants are forced to shop for provisions in company stores where prices are extremely inflated. Soap that is normally four bars for a dollar might be sold at a dollar a bar.

Puerto Rican migrant farmers are often separated from their families for up to six months of the year. The functional illiteracy of many migrants contributes to the sense of family isolation because they are unable to exchange letters with family and friends back home. If a migrant farmer is fired for not following the camp rules, he or she is at a loss in the United States because of the language barrier. Often, migrant farmers in this situation do not know where to go to receive help because they cannot read or speak English well enough. They usually end up homeless.[24]

Between 1982 and 1984, a total of $140 billion was cut from domestic social service programs by the Reagan administration. In the same period, large corporations received huge government research subsidies and even a reduction in federal income taxes.[25] Over one half of the cuts in this period of time were made in income maintenance programs that serve the needs of the poor. The Puerto Rican poor have lost much of the housing subsidies, health care benefits, and food stamps that at least helped to minimize the anguish of their marginal existence.

The reversal of the social responsibility trend sparked by the New Deal years of Franklin D. Roosevelt has resulted in an increase in the ranks of the poor. Today a large portion of the homeless are single men and women between the ages of twenty-five and thirty-five. In addition, families make up another large percentage of the homeless population. Shantytowns have been appearing in many towns and cities throughout the nation, but very little attention has been paid to this new social phenomenon by the news media. The welfare hotels where many of the Puerto Rican poor are forced to live—at an incredible cost to the public—are seldom mentioned on the evening news.

The economic reasons underlying the dismantlement of the so-called welfare state can be summarized in three points. First, the budgets of social service programs were cut because there was little opposition coming from the poor. Second, income maintenance programs were slashed in order to reduce the bargaining power of workers with employers. Third, the economic reorganization initiated between 1978 and 1987 was intended to redistribute the nation's wealth in an upward direction.[26]

Psychological Issues: A Shooting Gallery

The fatalism of the Puerto Rican community of the barrio is not a Latino psychological trait, as some Anglos have argued. Instead, it masks the reality of the feeling of powerlessness. The lack of social, economic, and political power is often expressed symptomatically as fatalism. One must become acquainted with life in the barrio in order to understand the psychology of persons who live there.

Rudy, my older brother, had a fairly normal childhood until the age of ten. Our parents divorced at that time after many years of marriage and struggle in a neighborhood composed predominantly of Irish, Italian, and Jewish people. The divorce made Rudy feel helpless and caused a strong rebellious reaction in him. Institutionalized authority became a negative symbol; he redefined his life by throwing himself into the street culture. Rudy became a junkie, and the shooting galleries became his local bar. Rudy substituted the needle for the family life he yearned to know.

I often went with him to a shooting gallery when I visited him in the South Bronx. When Rudy arrived at the building, he walked up the flight of steps to knock on Manolo's door. "It's me—Rudy," he said. "*Vaya*, Manny, I wanna use your works for a taste."

Manny normally charged junkies two dollars to use his works—drug paraphernalia—but a taste of dope was also acceptable as payment. Manny had needles, syringes, and eyedroppers enough to please the wishes of any junkie. Rudy entered a room that was already busy with junkies dangling needles from their veins. A few acknowledged that Rudy had entered the room. The apartment was poorly lit except for the area around the table where the junkies prepared their shots of dope. Above that table, a crucifix with the tragic figure of Jesus was hanging, imaging defeat. Jesus appeared to be looking down at the table, but no one noticed. Manny had nailed a Puerto Rican and an American flag on either side of the crucifix.

Rudy prepared his shot. The crucifix never drew his attention. The flags hung above his head like unused bathroom towels. He asked Manny for the big needle; it was the only one capable of piercing his leatherlike tracks. That needle was named "the spike." Rudy could hardly wait to feel the comforting embrace of la Señora Heroína. He placed the needle into his vein and watched the blood burst into the clear solution of dope in the eyedropper. A rush came over his entire body. Once again he felt good.

Over time, several families took Rudy into their homes.

He lived in Puerto Rico for several months, but returned to New York City's street culture and drug addiction. Only the street seemed capable of comforting his pain and profound sense of alienation. As a junkie, Rudy was forced to assume a life of petty crime, which made him a frequent visitor to the Tombs (jail). A psychology of impotence possessed Rudy's inner world.

Rudy lived on the streets. At times he lived with me when I was in seminary and at the Church of All Nations. I was never able to convince him to stop shooting dope and enter a drug rehabilitation program. I visited Rudy following Easter Sunday services on April 7, 1985. We had dinner together and talked about our childhood. That evening I received a telephone call from a police officer, who told me that my brother was dead. He was found lying on the sidewalk. The cause of death was later determined to be cirrhosis of the liver. He was thirty-one years old.

Rudy's feelings of alienation and cultural fragmentation were displaced in the drug culture. He did not fit into the biracial structure of U.S. society, which added to his feelings of being an outsider. The psychological perspective of the Anglo culture fails to understand people like Rudy.

The Puerto Rican community places race in a subordinate position to cultural identity; however, the biracial structure of U.S. society has caused many Puerto Ricans to adopt the racist attitudes of white society. Deep psychological scars are the result. Some Puerto Rican families have members with varying degrees of skin color. Thus, racist attitudes can lead to serious levels of family alienation. Puerto Rican children can also suffer low self-esteem as a result of an inability to handle either Spanish or English. This is particularly true of children raised in the United States. Fortunately, the future is beginning to look brighter for Puerto Ricans and other Latinos, given the influence of grass-roots organizations in the barrio that are working to resolve some of these issues. The church will be expected to play a major role in the life of the community in the future

SPANISH IN SPANGLISH

the words in our mouths
we cannot claim to possess.
they've been given to learn,

it is the law, just as Spanish words
before them were given. both pronounce
the victory that subjects. America

came in "friendship" claiming us
a spoil of war, Spain could no longer
argue the point, and we rejoiced thinking

ourselves free. they brought their laws,
words, promises to claim our Borinquén
while never once acknowledging us.

they said we could not govern and
theirs was a holy mission. they teach
us by breaking our backs; our sweat has

made them rich. they bathe on our beaches,
violate our women, but we remember what
Betances said: "They cannot give us what

they do not have."

3

Pastoral Reflections
on Hidden Dimensions

North Atlantic Christians agree that God is active in human history. However, many have difficulty relating to the biblical revelation of a God who chooses the side of the poor and oppressed in history. The exodus story in the Old Testament is the creative center of the Bible. It tells how God chose the side of oppressed Hebrew slaves who had suffered cruelly in Egypt. The New Testament tells how the Word became flesh in the person of Jesus, who was born in poverty and raised in an oppressed part of the known world, and who preached good news to the poor. The biblical story speaks of a God who is partial to the poor and oppressed. This chapter will be a pastoral reflection on scripture and the tradition in order to recover the hidden dimension of God's partiality toward the poor and oppressed.

The Poor in the Old Testament

The protection of the poor and defenseless was considered to be a social responsibility in the ancient Near East. The Hebrews were not the originators of compassionate social policy, although they are credited with locating this ethical concern within the cult and in covenant theology. The poor, the widowed, and the orphaned were singled out as groups in need of special protection in the legal and wisdom literature of Mesopotamia, Egypt, and Canaan. The same groups are mentioned in the Old Testament, especially in the preexilic prophetic literature.[1] In the ancient Near East, protection of these groups attested to the piety and virtue of gods and kings.

In the Old Testament, Yahweh (God) is the supreme defender of the poor and the oppressed. There are three primary legal codes in Israel that dictate in favor of the poor: the Book of the Covenant (Exodus 20:22–23:33), the Deuteronomic Code (Deuteronomy 12–26), and the Holiness Code (Leviticus 17–26). The desert life of the early Israelites was partly responsible for the development of an egalitarian ethic. Life in the desert required organization into close social units. An individual would find it impossible to live independently under the brutal conditions of the desert. Therefore, people organized into natural communities made up of families and clans. These units joined together to form tribes. The stranger, the widow, and the orphan were the persons most likely to live on the fringes of society and thus be in need of special protection. The legal codes of Israel make mention of these three groups as set apart for special protection by God.[2]

The principle of social equality forged in desert life was kept alive in the more settled urban life of Canaan in the cultic celebrations of Israel. For instance, the celebration of the Feast of Firstfruits (Weeks or Shavuot) recalls the story of Israel's liberation and establishment as a nation. Deuteronomy 26:5–9 is customarily read as a part of this celebration. It is sometimes seen as a confessional statement that encompasses all the major themes of the Torah and the book of Joshua. The people of Israel recollect their past in order not to forget their origins under oppression.[3] Just treatment of the stranger, the orphan, and the widow was expected by God as a part of the celebration. The religion of Yahweh unified the old pastoral-nomadic codes by successfully integrating them into the theology of the covenant. Integrating the desert sense of social responsibility into theology had two important functions. First, the elder who once uttered the codes was replaced by Yahweh, who represented absolute authority over the covenant people. This meant that the stranger, the widow, and the orphan were under divine protection. Second, Yahweh's law was heard by a people forever obligated to live in relation to the God who saved them.[4]

In Canaan the economic reality of Israel changed significantly over time. Property had belonged to the entire community in desert life, but it was becoming increasingly private. Wealth became concentrated in the hands of certain individuals, producing a widening gulf between the rich and the poor. (See 1 Sam. 8:14; 2 Sam. 24:19ff.; 1 Kings 16:24; Isa. 5:8.) The development of the monarchy further intensified this emergent social trend.[5] The city was home to a privileged class who enjoyed the protection of the king. Meanwhile, the countryside and the edges of the city became home to a marginalized population that provided goods and services for the dominant members of society. The poor simply grew poorer under those conditions.

Although the legal codes required that the rights of the poor, the widow, and the orphan be protected (see Ex. 21:1–11; 22:20–27), the privileged members of society did not often attend to legislation favoring the poor. Instead, wealth was concentrated within their particular class. The new administrative organization introduced into Israelite life in Canaan brought a new ingredient to national life: namely, economic development. This ingredient produced social inequalities and a turning away from the stipulations of the covenant forged in the desert (see 1 Kings 5:13–18; 9:15–22). The prosperity made possible under the monarchy rested on slavery, exploitation, forced labor, and high taxation.[6] The regulations found in Leviticus 25:8–55 regarding the year of jubilee represent an attempt to correct the negative impact of economic development in Israel's life. Every fifty years the Israelites were to implement God's socioeconomic revolution in Canaan in order to avoid extremes of poverty and wealth. The year of jubilee was patterned after the original exodus liberation event. It called for the freeing of slaves and debtors; their return to the ancestral land, implying a redistribution of wealth; and the resting of the land. Freedom is the fundamental framework of the jubilee legislation.[7] Scholars have debated whether such provisions were ever carried out. Yet God's people are still called to strive for the realization of this vision of the radical renewal of society.

Overall, the shift from desert life to stable existence under the monarchy caused the following changes. First, the shift to a stable agricultural economy resulted in a landless class. Second, the assimilation of aspects of Canaanite culture displaced traditional kinship notions forged in the desert. Third, a money economy took the place of a barter system of exchange. Fourth, the centralization of life in the city created economic inequalities and a decrease in social solidarity. Fifth, the Hebrew tribal organization was left in shambles, causing unemployment, extreme poverty, and conditions of wretchedness among the majority of the people.[8] The legal codes address these conditions in light of the concern to bring about renewed covenantal relationships in society.

The Prophets Briefly Considered

Prophetic literature represents a rich collection of material in which the poor and oppressed figure prominently. The prophets were concerned with improving the social status of marginal groups. They were consumed with a passion for justice that focused on the defense of the poor and oppressed in Israelite society.[9] Traditionally it has been argued that the prophets were merely concerned with creating a pure form of Israelite religion, monotheism, rejecting other gods. (See Isaiah 45:5–6; Hosea 2; Jeremiah 2:20–32.) According to this view, the prophets wished to purge the sacrificial cult system of its distortions, false worship, and unqualified support for those in power. In other words, the prophets anticipated that a moral transformation of society would result from a revitalized sacrificial system.[10]

The traditional understanding of the prophetic concern as a drive for moral purity and cultic renewal has come under review. This focus on purely moral issues tends to remove the prophets from their concrete social, political, and economic setting. Traditional scholarship tended to focus on psychological interpretations of the prophetic mission to the detriment of sociological factors. The prophets were perceived more as puritans than as revolutionary figures.[11] Actually, the prophets exercised at least four functions in society. First, they were interpreters of the times. Second, they were advocates of the poor. Third, they were critics of the status quo. Fourth, they were visionaries of social transformation based on the original covenant.

Isaiah, Jeremiah, Amos, Hosea, and Micah were more revolutionary than puritan in spirit; indeed, they proclaimed a radical political message that criticized the abuses of established power. Whether reform or abolition of the sacrificial cult was their mission, their message challenged the cultic institutions. Moreover, it is clear that the sociopolitical goals of the prophets were to advocate the rights of the poor as well as improve the overall situation of marginal groups in Israel.[12] The prophets Amos and Jeremiah engaged in what today would be considered "political treason." By attacking the cult, they also assaulted the monarchy and the state. In fact, the Temple was a patriotic symbol in Israelite national life. It held together the cultic symbol system uniting the diverse groups that comprised Israel. Hence, prophetic utterances against the cult were viewed by the establishment as treason.

Jeremiah's foes believed him to be a traitor. The priest Amaziah charged Amos with political treason. Jeremiah and Amos were not interested in reforming the government or correcting its abuses of power. Their goal was to overturn it because it was too corrupt to benefit from reformist measures. The national government was to be replaced by an egalitarian administration that had revived the stipulations of the covenant on which the people's life

originally rested.[13] The prophets actually stand out as revolutionary figures within the life of established Israel.

The New Testament:
Considered from a Single Angle of Vision

The New Testament contains God's promises to humanity, especially the poor and oppressed. The poor and oppressed are placed at the very center of salvation history
(Luke 4:18–19), but this dimension historically has been
glossed over by the established church. The good news
intended for the poor has undergone distortions in the
context of the North Atlantic world. To recover the meaning of Jesus' message of God's good news to the poor, some
understanding of the context of his time is helpful.

First-century Palestine was dominated by the Roman
empire. In 63 B.C. Pompey and the Roman legions took
control of Palestine. The region was made a part of Syria,
with a Roman proconsul as the representative of Rome.
The office of high priest was politicized by the appointment of a Hasmonean rather than one of the Zadokites,
the traditional family of high priests.[14] Thus, Roman
power ruled the affairs of Jewish life. The Roman legions
in Palestine protected the commercial interests of the empire. Slaves were used to work the land, which passed
from the hands of peasants to the estates of wealthy no-
bles.

Since the Jewish people did not have their own political
rulers, the Temple became the focus of their national life.
Its officials were responsible for collecting tribute from the
villages. Thus the Temple itself became an instrument of
Roman control. Actually, the priestly class had been dominant for centuries, using religious ideology to justify their
position.[15] Clearly, Herod and the Roman authorities recognized this function of the priestly class; therefore the
exploitation and control of the Jewish villages was carried
out peacefully by allowing the Temple to continue to function in society.

Jewish liberation movements arose, inspired by the promises of deliverance uttered by the prophets. The primary groups were the Essenes, the Sadducees, the Pharisees, the Zealots, and the Jesus movement. The Essenes were critical of the illegitimate priesthood and concerned with the purity of the Temple. The Sadducees accommodated Roman rule as part of their strategy for national restoration. The Pharisees believed the fulfillment of the Law of Moses in its entirety was necessary to realize national liberation. The Zealots were a military movement whose restoration strategy called for direct confrontation with Roman militarism. The Jesus movement determined that the main barrier to the kingdom of God was the Temple and the class reality that dominated its life.[16]

Social class conflict was a factor in the thinking of the various Jewish movements. Rome was linked to Palestine by way of the Temple economy, in the form of heavy taxation of the Jewish people. Palestinian farmers suffered much hardship due to the state-temple tax. Slave labor devalued wages for the skilled and unskilled workers of the cities of Palestine. Many of the economically destitute joined the Zealots in an attempt to struggle against a system that caused economic despair.[17]

Jesus' message took on important dimensions for the poor in the context of Roman-occupied Palestine. Jesus' movement sought to overcome the alienating structures of society by attacking the Temple and its priestly class domination (see Luke 19:45). Jesus began his popular mission in the countryside, where he implemented a long process of "conscientizing" the Jewish people about their own levels of oppression and estrangement from God. (See Luke 4:18–19; 6:20–25; 12:15–21; 13:22; and 18:31.) Jesus' message revived the egalitarian ideals of the desert tradition and called for an end to the class structure that benefited the few over the poor majority. Clearly, Jesus' ministry evolved in three stages. First, Jesus gathered his followers from the region of Galilee. He healed the sick and fed the hungry along the way. Second, Jesus and his followers passed through the towns, religious centers, and hamlets on their way to Jerusalem, raising the people's awareness about the challenge of the kingdom of God to the present situation of life. Third, Jesus ended his ministry by entering Jerusalem and attacking the economic base of the Temple.[18] The poor and oppressed gained a new champion in the person of Jesus, who announced the inbreaking of God's kingdom in a world structured to promote oppression for the many. The kingdom will be established on earth for all humanity, especially the poor and oppressed (see Luke 6:20; Matt. 5:4).

The exaltation of the poor in the message of Jesus should not be confused with the romanticization of poverty. God loves the poor but hates poverty. The Christian message radically calls into question the supposed permanence of the social structures that cause poverty and dehumanize people. The good news of Jesus calls the people of God to stand with the poor and oppressed in their struggle to transform the social order.

The Early Church and the Poor

The poor were the center of the first-century church's theology, because much of the membership of the early Christian community consisted largely of powerless and propertyless persons (1 Cor. 1:26–31). The book of Acts describes the early Christians as primarily humble or poor persons who had varying amounts of possessions, which they shared (Acts 2:42–47; 4:32–5:11). The evidence suggests that the Jerusalem community did not include persons with significant social influence and power.[19]

The Christian community developed a changed outlook toward the poor as it began to take in some of the wealthier members of Roman society during the second and third centuries. The radical demands of Jesus' message calling for solidarity with the poor and a rejection of the economics of exploitation and oppression lost its position of dominance (Luke 12:13–21; 18:18–30). The church fathers attempted to keep alive the radical teaching of Jesus, the experience of the Jerusalem church, and the ethic of solidarity with the poor characteristic of the letter of James. However, the church's success with the upper classes forced it to accommodate the life-style of the wealthy. Church teaching on the subject of poverty became more theoretical and focused on the practice of charity. The root causes of poverty went largely unexamined as the church assimilated into the social system of the Roman empire.[20]

The harmonization of Roman society and Christianity was completed in the early fourth century when Constantine declared Christianity to be the new state religion. The church's full assimilation into imperial society meant that the radical nature of the gospel and its challenge to imperial society's systemic injustice was omitted from the concerns of official theology. The poor and oppressed were made voiceless by the new version of "royal theology" being advocated by such thinkers as Eusebius of Caesarea. However, the church's assimilation into Roman society was met with the radical reaction of monasticism, which sought to keep alive the authentic message of the gospel. For instance, Basil of Caesarea severely criticized the empire's system of economic growth that made social inequality a way of life. He regularly spoke out against the upper-class practice of accumulating wealth unjustly. Basil believed that human wickedness was the basis of the pursuit of private capital at the expense of the poor. Wealth was to be used to serve the poor, whom God favors.[21]

The monastic reaction to the harmonization of church and state was not meant to idealize poverty. Instead, the movement intended to represent a radical critique of enculturated Christianity by its embodiment of the prophetic and apostolic richness of biblical faith. Clearly, the church has lived over the centuries with a certain tension between royal and prophetic theological expressions, dating back to the Constantinian synthesis of Christianity and classical culture.[22] However, it remains clear that the poor and oppressed were the privileged recipients of the good news of Jesus of Nazareth. Jesus was one of the poor from the hill country of Judea (Luke 1:65). He identified himself with the prophets of Israel and stood over against the royal theological tradition. He revealed the reign of God to the rich through his identification with the poor and oppressed, who served as God's instrument of judgment and grace.

Spanish Christianity in the New World

Between the time of Constantine's official embrace of Christianity and the sixteenth-century colonization of Latin America, there were repeated challenges to enculturated Christianity. For example, in the late Middle Ages popular movements arose to question the synthesis between Christianity and the empire. The Waldensian movement identified with the poor and held the rich and powerful responsible for the social evils of the day. The Franciscan and Dominican movements likewise challenged society's oppressors. During the sixteenth-century colonization of Latin America by Spain and Portugal, the priest Bartolomé de Las Casas raised a prophetic voice against enculturated Christianity's justification of the enslavement of native people.

The sixteenth-century conquest and colonization of the so-called New World resulted in the greatest concentration of dehumanizing labor ever known in the West. Roughly 70 million Amerindians and 40 million Africans were sacrificed on the altar of North Atlantic economic expansionism. Capitalism was born in their trail of tears and blood. Religion blessed the Spanish conquest and colonization of all the coasts and lands of the New World. The Spanish conquest of most of Central and South America can be viewed as a study in the manipulation of state religion. The Spanish version of Christianity played at least two roles in the colonial project. First, it made the entire colonial project a holy event. Second, religion itself was turned into one of the instruments of domination.[23] The pursuit of wealth to finance the economic revolution taking place in Europe meant a brutal and dehumanizing experience for the enslaved native and African peoples in the New World.

The populations of Central and South America were subjected to a process of cruel cultural dislocation that included the elimination of leaders, the destruction of native institutions, and a total collapse of local economies. The myths, values, and worldviews of the Spanish conquistadores were superimposed on the enslaved native people. Thus, conquest and colonization meant for native people both the loss of their land and a clear spiritual genocide.[24]

Works of art produced by the peoples of Central and South America in the seventeenth and eighteenth centuries, following the Spanish conquest, reflect that sense of spiritual genocide, surrender, and defeat. They include many images of Christ in suffering and defeat. The Amerindians located their existential reality within these Christological images, which represented their life under colonialism. The colonial church was not a defender of the rights of the poor and oppressed. A few prophets, among them Bartolomé de Las Casas, emerged in the wilderness of Spanish Catholicism to defend the rights of enslaved native persons but they were few and far apart. The church ignored the gospel's requirement of justice toward the enslaved and exploited serfs of colonial society.

The Spanish empire began to decline in the eighteenth century, making it possible for Latin American nations to assert their desire for independence. A complete break from the Spanish crown occurred during the first half of the nineteenth century. Between 1810 and 1850, national liberation was the dominant theme and goal of the nations of Latin America. But the new centers of political and economic power that emerged for the former Spanish colonies turned out to be the United States and Great Britain. Protestantism was encouraged in these new countries as part of the modernization project. The new religious ethos facilitated the break with the traditional feudal-based society characteristic of the Spanish colonial experiment. The Spanish Catholic church was displaced from its role as mediator of the divine–human encounter. The feudal orientation, which placed the church and the landlords at the top of the social hierarchy, was replaced by the Protestant focus on the authority of the individual in a modern liberal capitalist society.

The Spanish Catholic church continues to have a significant institutional presence in Latin America. However, it has lost a great deal of its power within society since the mid-nineteenth century. National emancipation in Latin America under the influence of the Protestant capitalist ideology has meant for the Spanish Catholic church banishment to the private or personal dimension of life. Indeed, Protestantism did not appeal to the local ruling class as a personal religion. But the Protestant concept of the person as a free moral agent undergirded the effort of the newly emancipated societies to break free of the oppressive demands of the Spanish Catholic church and its medievalist clerics. So while claiming their ancestral ties to the Catholic Church, the new ruling class embraced the new relationship with the Protestant ethos of the United States and Great Britain. They moved into positions left open by the former colonial elite. The new ideology based on the Protestant ethic—an inner sense of duty, responsibility, industry, moderation, frugality, and honesty—laid the foundation for a new colonial order bearing the marks of dependent capitalism.

But the freedom under the new centers of power—the United States and Great Britain—came with a price. Freedom actually meant the right of the United States and Great Britain to do business, exploit cheap labor, and extract primary resources from Latin America. The local oligarchies benefited from the socioeconomic arrangement of the new colonial order. But the radical message of the gospel was domesticated to serve the ruling interests. The Latin American masses were steadily pushed further into poverty and wretchedness.

The Spanish Catholic church, representing the old colonial social order, has attempted repeatedly to regain some of its lost influence in Latin American society. It was placed on the defensive because it no longer played the role of sacralizing, for the ruling elite, the social and economic order in the new world. Once it lost this function, it became a reactionary institution. The ruling class in Latin America were aware that Protestantism was lending a new religious justification to the process of neocolonialism. While two versions of religion were thus struggling for the favor of the ruling elites of Latin America, an undercurrent of popular religion began to develop.

Popular Religion

Popular religion—popular Catholicism, spiritism, Pentecostalism, and the Christian base communities—represents an undercurrent in Latin American society that has incubated the liberation sentiments of the dispossessed masses. The Latin American poor reacted to traditional religiosity by turning to forms of spiritual life that nurtured a faith expression relevant to their struggles against marginalization, oppression, and general conditions of wretchedness. The Christian base communities arising in the mid-twentieth century represent one of the more significant versions of popular religion in Latin American society. Popular religion can be viewed as the poor's protest movement. It originates in the material concerns of the oppressed majority who are dislocated from the political and economic structures of society. Theology and concrete reality are unified in popular religious thought. Protestant and Roman Catholic versions of popular religion hold up Jesus' identification with the poor and his prophetic message of social transformation on behalf of those living on the margins of society.

In its positive forms, popular religion has a number of

functions. First, it provides a symbol system that enables the poor to understand their suffering and project hope. Second, it connects persons to both the material and the spiritual dimensions of life. Third, it enables persons to experience a deep sense of community that naturally grows out of worship life. Fourth, it perceives religion as an essential part of social life, rather than as a way of avoiding the real world. Fifth, its believers experience a sense of process and change that connects to their desire for a more just social order. Sixth, theology is harmonized with the collective concerns of the poor so as to promote solidarity and mutual self-help projects. Seventh, an organic perception of faith emerges for the poor that interconnects God, nature, and humanity in a positive way.[25] In short, positive forms of popular religion tend not to idealize the content of faith but to relate it to the concrete present and future hope of the poor who keep alive the gospel's vision of a new social order.

Latin American popular religion represents the poor's reappropriation of Jesus' message of hope and liberation. Liberation theology was given birth by popular religion, while official religion in Latin America struggled to conserve its position with the status quo. However, the Latin American religious community in the United States has evolved somewhat independently of the popular religious tradition on the other side of the Rio Grande. First, a strong sense of historical impotence inspired a theology of passive submission to white society. Second, the Latino religious community in the United States tended to escape social reality by retreating into a personal inner dimension that rested on the faith perspective of the Latin American colonial heritage.

Liberation Theology

Liberation for the Latino poor means that the theological efforts of the church will be devoted to interpreting the material conditions of a people so as to open the way for their possible change. Liberation theology for Latinos in the United States demands that people pledge themselves to service and commitment within history. The strategies of commitment envision a transformation of the given social structure within which Latino people live, seeking a more humane social order. The new order will keep the needs of the poor in mind at all points of social planning and development. The Latino church in the United States cannot afford to follow North Atlantic theological criteria that keep one personally neutral before history. Rigorous social, economic, political, historical, and cultural analysis must be part of its theological method. Latinos in the United States religious community must rediscover God and Christ as the liberators of human history on behalf of the poor and oppressed.

Liberation theology, as a theology of social transformation, relates God's Word of promise to the present situation of a people living in wretchedness and searching for a sign of God's judgment in history. The divine Word of judgment and promise can be seen in liberation movements such as the homesteading groups on the Lower East Side of Manhattan or the Central American and South African solidarity groups throughout the United States. Liberation movements like these represent a certain political engagement directed to the service of God's Word of justice on behalf of the poor. The Latino church in the United States must devote itself to the notion that humanity was created in the image of God for freedom (Gen. 1:26)—not to be dominated. This expression of the church universal must be prepared to say no to all forms of cultural, political, economic, social, and theological domination that promote dehumanization in the Latino community.

The liberation theology endeavor should be seen against the background of popular religion and in the context of world economics as it existed in the 1950s. The nations of the world were divided into the developed and the underdeveloped countries. The dominant economic theory maintained that the underdeveloped or Third World nations had to follow the historical path of the North Atlantic nations in order to shed their inferior economic status. In the 1960s, the theory of development lost all credibility in the Third World because it did not address the legacy of colonialism or the reality of neocolonialism. In fact, the underdevelopment of Latin America reflects the last five hundred years of North Atlantic domination. Liberation theology examines the injustice of the North Atlantic's "misdevelopment" of Central and South America. Thinking, speaking, and acting in terms of liberation define the horizon of theological thought.[26]

Underdevelopment and neocolonialism have been prime factors in Latin American society leading to a growing Latino population in the United States. The root causes of migration to the North are economic, social, political, and cultural dependence on the North Atlantic world. Liberation theology asserts that a radical and abrupt departure from the vicious cycle of dependence can transform the life of the poor. The Latino church in the United States needs to develop a historically conditioned faith through which it can examine the dynamic of "underdevelopment" in the United States. Latino poverty in the United States must be understood as a by-product of the economic structures and class reality operating in the Latino communities of North, South, and Central America.

The Latino church in the United States must reflect on its role in North Atlantic society in light of the experience of oppression in white society. It must discover the political import of God's preferential option for the poor. It must serve as a light for others, enabling white society to see the context of the barrio and the human disfigurement it represents. Christ died to give life to the wretched poor, he eats at the table of the hungry, spills his blood with the little girl shot to death by a stray bullet from a drug pusher's gun, bears in his arm the needle tracks of those who have repeatedly injected themselves with dope, and stands on the dehumanizing welfare lines located in the barrio. The God who has thus identified with the poor and oppressed in Jesus Christ is to be adored by the Latino church in the United States, and that church must be ready to exercise its prophetic vocation in the context of the larger society.

HOME STREET

*broken glass, bottle caps, asphalt blacktop commune
as silent streets in repressed violence remain
victims of loneliness.
ebony-skinned and curly-haired a Latino boy stands
by 1203, his stoop, eating sugarcane.*

*a corner knows the passage of time if not of us.
it mirrors death, soaks up murderous blood. knives
leave sheaths and enter bodies as machetes
fell cane. bodies drop, spilling blood,
another infamous story of the block.*

*city morgues fill with emptied hearts,
a corner speaks of such in silence.*

*days without yester . . . like motherless boys
half-lit blocks survive, disdained shamed
half burnt out and yet the pigeons fly by
unburdened, careless, like a Latino dream.*

*"Pee Wee, you're dead!" was it the corner took
your life, the prison of your kind? or the knife?
were you so emptied? your Latin ebony is gone
white ice, the corner your memoriam.*

*empty streets empty feeling, if such can be barren
in their reach stretching to arrive,
lost inside of searching's places.*

4

Transformation in the Parish

The Church of All Nations of the Lower East Side of Manhattan represents one Latino congregation attempting to address the reality of poverty in an affluent society. I was completing my last year of theological studies at Union Theological Seminary in 1981 when I was appointed to serve as pastor of that church. The United Methodist district superintendent told me that the local charge was in need of congregational renewal and there was a slight tenant problem to be resolved. What I actually discovered was a congregation living in a state of despair and membership decline. The church had been part of the East Side Parish, founded in 1903 when the Lower East Side was "more Jewish than Jerusalem." Frank Mason North immortalized the parish and its mission in the hymn "Where Cross the Crowded Ways of Life." North also suggested to the first pastor, William Stone, that the parish be renamed. Since the building was used by a multinational community during the early part of this century, the church was renamed the Church of All Nations. The Spanish-speaking charge was established in 1955, and it is the only worshiping community left of five.

When I arrived to take charge of the congregation, only eight members were at worship. The church was in a state of utter chaos. I found a collection of unpaid bills, a note from the City Marshal threatening to remove the gas and electric meters, and five different bank accounts no one knew anything about, and the "tenant problem" was draining the congregation's energy. The church did not have any source of operating income other than the Sunday offering. The Annual Conference was subsidizing its ministry quite heavily; however, this amounted to salary supplements for the pastor because there were no programs functioning except a dying Welfare Advocacy program. That effort had been left behind by the English-speaking congregation, which disbanded in February 1981. The congregation had not even enjoyed the benefit of a strong liturgical life or music for worship.

The lay leader lackadaisically introduced me to the eight members of the church who showed up for worship on my first Sunday. There was so much hurt and disillusionment in the church that little time was available for ritualizing the installation of the new pastor. The church was suffering from neglect, low self-esteem, and a strong feeling of abandonment. I stepped into the pulpit quite unsure about what the future held for us. I had to ask myself, "Do I belong in this church?" The power of the gospel to transform a deadening social reality was a source of comfort to me. The road that opened up before me that morning called for the healing of pain and deep hurts caused by the experience of neglect felt by the church. The question of the social meaning of faith in that worshiping community could not be addressed immediately. My initial ministry would have to revolve around healing the community, organizing the church finances, paying bills, raising funds, and finding a solution to the tenant problem.

The Church of All Nations was renting out three rooms on the fourth floor of its building. Two rooms were rented to students, and the third to a couple. It was the couple who gave the church all its trouble. An elderly member of the congregation had recommended them to the church as reliable tenants. She was not aware that the couple had a drug problem. Dee was a multiple drug abuser, and Tommy was a heavy pot smoker and professional bodybuilder. (He once held the title of "Mr. America.") The couple had not paid any rent to the church in over a year; indeed, Tommy ("Mr. America") had the nasty habit of physically threatening any person who dared to question him about the situation. He was known to have pulled doors right out of their frames when angry. The former pastor had refused to go up to the fourth floor of the building because he feared that the "slight tenant problem" would break his neck.

The South Bronx prepared me to deal with many unusual situations. (I have always wondered whether this constituted one of the reasons behind my appointment to the church.) I organized a tenants' meeting on the fourth floor of the building to announce that the church would no longer rent out residential space. The persons living on the fourth floor were given the remainder of the summer to move out. Tommy was told that it did not matter whether the past rent had been paid or not. One of the residents of the fourth floor, a skinny Hare Krishna disciple, shared a story about Tommy with me after the meeting. One evening, Tommy crashed into the poor kid's room by literally breaking down the door. He picked up the innocent vegetarian and placed him against the wall. "You better move out of here or I am going to kill you, you freak," said Tommy. The young disciple was terrified by the incident and after this scene chose only to store his possessions in the room.

I called a second tenants' meeting to look into the progress being made toward moving. That evening someone dumped a gallon of paint on the front steps of the building. Small droplets of paint were scattered on the front of the building extending down from the top floor, indicating that the spill had probably come from the roof. The circumstantial evidence all pointed to Tommy as the culprit. I went upstairs and confronted him. "Did you see anything strange last night? I noticed you sitting on the steps across the street. Some idiot dumped an entire gallon of paint on the church steps. If I catch the person who did it . . . !" We exchanged angry looks.

"I didn't see nothing. It must have been the freaky dickies"—his term for the neighborhood punk rockers. "You got to watch those people. The freaky dickies did it." Again, we stared angrily at each other.

"Let me tell you something, Tommy," I replied. "I am going to watch those freaky dickies like a hawk. If I catch them in the act, forget it."

Tommy was not going to move willingly. The fact that he never paid the church any rent made little difference to him. He believed it was his right to be housed in the building and he was willing to intimidate the church with his size and the .45 caliber pistol in his room. The church was forced to hire a lawyer and start eviction proceedings. A few weeks before the scheduled moving date Tommy again used the front steps to make a statement. About 2 A.M. I heard some very odd sounds coming into the bedroom from outside. I jumped out of bed and went to the window to determine the source of the noise. Mr. America was on the front steps emptying the contents of several large garbage bags. I put on my clothes, took a broom, and headed downstairs. Tommy was sitting on the bottom step when I started out the front door. He was playing dumb. I proceeded to sweep the garbage off the steps and right on top of him. That got him on his feet.

"Why did you do this to the church steps, Tommy?" I said. "The church has never treated you unfairly, but you insist upon abusing it. You have no respect for the congregation, which is making me real angry!"

Tommy was shaking his head apologetically. "Oh, I'm sorry, Harold! I just keep hearing in my head, 'Kill, kill, kill,' like in Vietnam. Man, I think of you like a brother." Tommy probably never went to Vietnam, but he enjoyed using his fantasy as a theatrical device.

"Tommy," I answered, "when you were going through Vietnam, I was living in the South Bronx. I watched many friends meet death at the end of a needle or the sharp point of a knife. Next time you hear, 'Kill, kill, kill,' find another set of steps. Don't do it here, understand? As for thinking of me like a brother: Brothers often fight. Our fight has yet to come."

Tommy spent the rest of the early morning hours running up and down the avenue with his girlfriend, mooning passing cars.

Tommy worked at a local movie house as a bouncer. When his moving day finally came, he was not able to take all his belongings on the first trip. Left behind were a sofa bed and a number of other items stored in the building. Tommy intended to pick them up a week later. I went upstairs to look over the rooms he had vacated, only to find the walls covered with vintage graffiti. Tommy had painted all kinds of messages to me. He illustrated the threat to kill me with primitive-style cartoon characters. He made a caricature of me with a bone through my nose, beneath which he had written, KILL HAROLD! The writing on the wall was meant as a personal challenge to me. Tommy's things were taken downstairs. A locksmith was called to change the lock on the front door of the building. I did not want Tommy to use his keys to come in and place a pistol to my head. I walked over to the movie house where he worked and informed him of the changes. Tommy was angry with me, particularly since I had discovered the writing on the wall sooner than he expected. "I'll be there tonight at six thirty to pick up the rest of my things," he said threateningly.

I knew Tommy would not show up by himself. He had not been able to intimidate me, so he was sure to arrive with some bodybuilding thugs. I placed a call to the local police station and informed them of the delicate situation. They promised to respond immediately should anything happen. I felt reassured, but I knew it would be necessary to deal with Tommy on his own terms. The old-fashioned way would put an end to the whole nightmare. I placed a few telephone calls to friends from the South Bronx. Two are jujitsu experts, and Joe was born a natural Samson. My friends had been following the Tommy situation for weeks. They were prepared to help the church at the drop of a hat. "What time do you want us to show up, Harold?"

"Come over at around six P.M. Mr. America will most likely show up soon after that with his bodybuilding gang," I told them.

A van pulled up to the front of the church building at exactly six thirty. The back door of the van was thrown open by the driver, letting out eight huge bodybuilders. One man had held the title of "Mr. International" for a year. Tommy's friends looked like a demolition-company wrecking crew. I was certainly hoping that God chooses sides with the weak. I figured either we were going to come out of the situation unhurt or all of us would be visiting the hospital. Clearly, only a real showdown could bring this oppressive episode to an end. The future of the congregation depended upon that evening's outcome. Tommy and his gang approached the steps. I thought to myself, Here we go, fellows.

We threw the front doors to the building wide open, allowing pedestrians a clear view of the church entrance. Tommy's pals looked Joe over with a great deal of curiosity. They were probably wondering how Joe managed to be so big. Joe was also wearing a leather jacket which tended to bulk out at the sides, making it appear that he was carrying pistols. Tommy's friends moved the sofa into the parked van, which was just at the bottom of the steps. Some of Tommy's weights had been stored in the church basement. If anything was going to happen, it would most likely be in the privacy of the basement. Joe and I escorted five of Tommy's gang downstairs. I unlocked the basement door, though I could not remember seeing any dumbbells down there. Once in the cellar, Tommy went directly to the boiler room, behind the furnace, to the place where his dumbbells were stored. He handed each of his friends a set of weights. There was a tense moment of silence, followed by a march back upstairs. I sighed with relief. For a moment it had appeared that we would come to blows in the basement. In my heart of hearts, I feared for the boiler more than my own health. My God, we'll ruin the furnace! I thought to myself. But the only thing that happened was that one of Tommy's pals announced he had to use the bathroom. You can hardly feel threatened by a bodybuilder who needs to relieve himself!

In single file, we marched back upstairs and out to the front of the building. Joe waited for the guy using the bathroom. It was obvious that Tommy was feeling very frustrated by the welcoming committee I had organized. He wanted a fight but could not be sure of the outcome. (I learned much later that Tommy was convinced my friends were hit men from my old neighborhood.) The entire affair ended that evening on the front steps of the church. We looked into one another's eyes. "Well, all I have to say to you is good luck," Tommy said with a note of threat in his voice.

"All I can say to you is good luck, too, Tommy," was my reply. He never came back to abuse either the church or its pastor.

The Sunday after Tommy's move was full of genuine celebration. After I announced that Mr. America had finally moved out of the building, members of the church shouted out with joy, thanking God for the victory. A very difficult part of the church's history had come to an end, enabling the people to move to new ground. The spiritual despair to which Tommy's presence in the building had contributed so much was transformed into hope. The elderly member of the congregation who had recommended the couple apologized to the church for doing so, but the lay leader assured her that she had nothing to be sorry about. She could not have known how it would turn out. The church perceived Tommy's departure as a time for renewal. The future ministry of the church slowly came into focus in terms of a renewed sense of Christian mission. The congregation reflected upon new ways of serving God, former members returned to worship, and the journey toward a social-witness faith began.

Notes on Transformation

We organized a work party to paint the rooms on the fourth floor. In future they would be used to house offices for worthwhile groups that were in need of space. In my sermons I began to combine private and corporate theological themes in order to encourage the congregation to broaden its commitment to the social gospel, and the administrative board made the fourth-floor space available to social justice organizations.

The first group to find a home in the Church of All Nations was Mobilization for Survival. They made a monthly contribution in lieu of rent that went toward the church's gas and electric bills. Moreover, this group helped the congregation to understand the peace issue.

In general, the peace movement is perceived in the Latino community as primarily a European and American middle-class concern. Mobilization for Survival enabled the congregation to see the connection between defense spending and the social situation of the impoverished community. Every dollar spent on arms is money taken away from programs designed to meet the needs of the poor, especially in the areas of housing, education, and health care. The church community was able to understand the dynamics of the peace issue in relation to the formation of the ghetto. Federal budget cuts in social service programs were seen as part of the move to increase military spending.

Mobilization for Survival, working with a coalition of peace groups from around the country, helped organize the nation's largest peace rally, held in Central Park on June 12, 1982. The Church of All Nations was at the heart of the effort because Mobilization played a key role in the entire event. Members of the congregation were enlisted to distribute flyers about the rally all over the Lower East Side. It was fascinating to discover how theological positions can be transformed through a change in the way one relates to the world. Many members of the church still clung to a privatized faith stance, but as they became actively involved with the peace issue a new theological understanding began to emerge for them. They no longer talked about peace in strictly personal or escapist terminology; rather, peace came to imply committed action and responsibility toward God's creation. The church newly defined as a community called to bring justice into the world.

Mobilization for Survival outgrew its space shortly after

the Central Park rally and moved to a new location. Within a few weeks the rooms were sought by another very interesting group. The new applicant was the Women's Ordination Conference (WOC). This group is made up of Roman Catholic nuns and lay women who advocate the ordination of women as priests. Although the churchwomen voted enthusiastically to let WOC use the space for another nominal contribution toward our operating expenses, some of the men felt less excited by the idea. What became clear in the debate was that ordination images Christ's humanity, not his masculinity. I thought the traditional values of the Latino community would impact negatively on the decision of the church, and WOC would be rejected as a tenant, but it was not. Their support for WOC enabled the women of the church to experience their own political strength.

By the time WOC moved to new headquarters in Washington, D.C., a year later, the group had helped the congregation take a closer look at the nature of a white-male-dominated church structure. I continued to integrate new theological themes and social justice issues in my sermons, hoping the church would invite more growth. Giving support to organizations doing social justice forms of ministry was crucial to making the transition from a private evangelical church to one seeking to become engaged in the life of the community. I hoped the church would go on to develop a more intentional program of action/reflection to challenge the assumptions of its traditional faith formulas. Developing a project was essential to the growth process that had started with our support for groups doing social-witness ministry.

The Center for Immigrants' Rights (CIR) was the next to occupy the fourth-floor space at the Church of All Nations. CIR exercised more influence over the congregation's theological growth and social action commitment than any other group. Through CIR the distance that once existed between the church and groups using the building diminished, and the congregation was able to become a part of a growing network of immigrants' rights advocates.

At the level of the local community, the church was instrumental in establishing a housing justice group on the Lower East Side as well. God's Word of radical transformation did break into the church's conservative and privatized faith landscape in a way that changed even the most traditional members of the worshiping community.

Change Came in Steps

As I pointed out in the first chapter, the members of the Spanish-speaking church were nurtured in a deeply evangelical tradition, which called for separating from the affairs of this world and maintaining the division between religion and politics. The Christian person was understood in terms of the ethic of self-control. God's kingdom was otherworldly and not to be harmonized with this fallen, sinful world. This faith posture is the legacy of the Puerto Rican colonial heritage, in which the missionary church implanted a theological tradition characterized by feelings of resignation and historical impotence.

The Church of All Nations learned to examine its colonial identity in a critical way. Through a long process of self-examination it has become one of the few Latino churches that understands the importance of social-witness ministry. The wretched conditions in which Latinos live is blamed on personal sin by the Pentecostal church. This explanation was simply not an acceptable one for us.

The geographical area that concerned the congregation was the Lower East Side of Manhattan. The largest concentration of Puerto Rican working poor live in this part of New York City, and the congregation's outreach efforts extended to them.

Many church members lived in public housing projects located on Avenue D and the East River. To get from their apartments to the church on Sunday morning meant a long walk, during which they were bombarded with images of neglect and destitution. Two faces predominate in the reality of the Lower East Side: the face of affluence and the face of abject poverty. The streets are lined with artists' studios, new wave bars, and fashionable cafés; at the same time abandoned tenements, parks filled with homeless people, drug houses, winos, and junkies are a part of the landscape. Faith is always challenged by the existence of such contrasting conditions. Members of the church have come to me in tears because no one would stop to help an unconscious wino lying on the sidewalk in a pool of blood. Tears would also fill their eyes when as they walked to church they saw little children standing by cracked windows in abandoned tenements.

Jesus ministered to outcasts, the poor, the sick, the homeless, the strangers, the oppressed, and those whom organized religion pushed aside. The Puerto Rican community of lower Manhattan was experiencing the kind of social alienation that grows out of a feeling of historical impotence. The overwhelming problems of the community made many feel helpless. Moreover, the dominant culture, white society, hardly recognizes the Latino presence or grapples with the problems of the Latino poor. This isolation tends to reinforce the situation of helplessness. The appeals of the Latino poor always seem to fall on deaf ears. The Church of All Nations began asking itself, What can we do to impact the life of the community? Key church leaders called a meeting to develop a plan of action to answer the question. The guiding image the church elected to use was that of change agent.

The Spirit of God was moving the Church of All Nations in new ways. The old faith formulas imported from Puerto Rico no longer explained the situation of oppression and racial and economic injustice. Anna, a thirteen-year-old member of the church, was on her way to worship one winter Sunday in the company of her mother. They lived on the other side of Tompkins Square Park and normally went around it on the way to Sunday services. That morning Anna and her mother decided to take a shortcut through the park. The brutal side of the nation's so-called "economic recovery" assaulted them. Anna discovered the reality of homelessness in a new way because a disturbing sight rattled her faith.

Just as they were about to leave the park, something attracted Anna's attention. An old wino was sitting on a park bench with a blanket covering his shoulders, protecting him against the cold winter air. He held a partially naked infant on his lap. The baby was crying at the very top of its lungs. The wino hardly noticed the infant's level of discomfort.

How did the baby get in the wino's lap? Anna wondered. Was it left behind by its mother? Did the wino find it in the park? Was it hurt? What should be done? Anna begged her mother to do something to save the infant, but her mother was afraid to act.

"I don't think we should tell the police," said her mother. "The bum might see us do it and follow us. We could get hurt!"

Anna simply could not live with inaction. "Pastor Harold would know what to do. I'm going to tell him. We can't just do nothing."

The parsonage doorbell rang and I came downstairs. Anna's eyes indicated that something terrifying had happened to her on the way to church. She recounted the experience, choking on her words. I could understand her mother's response. Her husband had been killed on the street in front of their apartment building a few years earlier, and thus she always felt it was better not to get involved. Anna and I called the police and urged them to investigate the situation and collect the infant. That morning I shared the incident with the rest of the congregation during the worship service. Anna's actions were applauded by the members of the church. Some of them believed Anna's action constituted a sign from God to the church indicating the command to act justly and mercifully to those in need. The baby was held up as a symbol of the helplessness of the Lower East Side's Latino poor, who needed the empowerment made possible by Good Samaritans. Anna showed the congregation how to walk with God on the road of compassion.

Anna's story was inspiring for the church. The congregation had talked about ways of reaching out, but Anna had shown them the necessity of action. Her concern moti-vated the congregation to call a meeting to define the relationship between the church and the community. At the meeting, four goals were chosen for implementation, goals that would result in the development of a more com-munity-engaged faith. First, the members of the church needed to clarify and develop the intellectual tools for examining the reality of Latino marginalization in light of the dynamics of classism, racism, and sexism. Second, it would be necessary to stimulate the development of lead-ership for the purpose of empowerment of the local Latino community. Third, ways of increasing the interac-tion between the congregation and the community would be established. Fourth, the congregation would embrace one or two specific areas for social action.

The congregation struggled over identifying different strategies to realize its goals. Some members felt that prayer was the only strategy necessary to bring about the changes desired. Others argued for the development of strategies that would include interaction between the community and biblical, social, political, and economic reflection. Upon reaching a consensus we charted the strategy for goal implementation in terms of three pro-grammatic components:

1. A film series. Films would be used to help persons develop a critical awareness of the impact of racism, sexism, and classism on the Latino community.
2. Educational forums. Community forums would be designed to reinforce the film series by building on the developing critical awareness and increasing community interaction.
3. Bible study. The scriptures would be examined both from the traditional literal viewpoint and from higher-critical perspectives.

The Christian base community model of action/reflection was used to facilitate growth in Christian social action. All three program components interacted simultaneously with each of the established goals.

Goal One: To clarify and develop the intellectual tools for examining the reality of Latino marginalization in light of the dynamics of classism, racism, and sexism. All three program components interacted with this goal. Vincent made an interesting suggestion to the church regarding Bible study and street services. He was well aware of the colonial past and the missionary legacy that made members of the church incapable of seeing the dynamics behind Latino marginalization. Vincent believed the most serious problem faced by the church centered around the question of the nature of biblical interpretation. The Latino evangelical tradition prevailing in the North American context continues to persuade people that faith has little to do with "worldly" matters. That tradition interprets faith in opposition to the world and its dynamics of racism, classism, and sexism. Private Christian faith and a personal relationship with God were all the Christian needed to think about; indeed, the Christian life was best expressed by attitudes of honesty, frugality, and hard work. In the traditional framework of interpretation, suffering was not seen in terms of conflict between elements of the larger society, especially conflict caused by the negative effects of racism, classism, and sexism on the Latino community. Vincent believed that the church needed a Bible study designed to permit members to examine the dynamics of discrimination with new interpretive lenses. He was dissatisfied with the faith formula that called for a resigned attitude in the face of human suffering. Vincent argued that a worship service in the park would help make Bible study come alive in the church and make faith a living reality in the streets.

Jesus can be seen as a paradigm for the street minister. He was seldom found in the Temple. Instead, countryside, roads, towns, and small villages became places of critical encounter for Jesus and his disciples. The laws of social convention were constantly set aside by him in favor of the needs of the oppressed and outcasts of official society. The people whom organized religion had rejected became Jesus' instruments of judgment and grace that criticized the established structure of racism, classism, and sexism. Jesus created a new community by gathering up the outcasts during the course of his street ministry. Mainline denominations are not noted for street-style ministry, but Vincent's suggestion to do a park service was received favorably.

Services were conducted in the Lower East Side Park. It represented a major move for the church, which was accustomed to hold services exclusively in the security of the sanctuary. Because the church held services in the street, the long process of developing an understanding of the causes of human suffering was begun. The worship service was held in the section of the park frequented most by junkies and drug pushers. Members of the congregation wanted to interact with junkies and pushers because they represented the most feared and despised persons of the community. Our people lived in fear of drug addicts, but they fearlessly handed out flyers about the church project. The pushers were the ones most disturbed. They wanted us to leave and made a number of threatening gestures, but the congregation was not going to be intimidated. We were determined to hold our prayer service bearing witness to God's transforming power. A week before, a junkie had been killed in the park. He was lifted up in prayer that morning by one of the lay preachers.

The park service caused many people to ask questions about the living conditions of the Latino poor. Why are people living under such horrid and oppressive conditions? The idea of mission developed as a major theme growing out of the park service. The church moved to experience itself as a sacramental community. We believed in the importance of bearing witness to God's presence in the world by becoming a community whose mission is to heal a larger community broken by racism, sexism, and classism. God's Word was gradually allowed to address the local community context with all its pain. Members of the church came to the realization that it is too easy to avoid dealing with the community's suffering within the stained-glass comfort of the sanctuary. The despair on the urban streets, the loss of children to heroin and crack, and the violence on the blood-stained corners would no longer permit the avoidance of reality.

The service in the park was a catalyst for a new level of critical social and biblical reflection that focused on the causes of human misery in the ghetto. A selection of scripture from the Gospel of Mark (the mission of the disciples, Mark 6:7–13) was read during a combination Bible study and brainstorming session and was related to the questions of racism, sexism, and classism. The congregation discerned how the disciples were charged with proclaiming the kingdom and ministering to the sick and outcast, and how their authority rested on faithfulness to their commission from Christ. One literalist in the group surprised me when she suggested that the disciples' power over unclean spirits could be understood in terms of oppressive social structures. Carmen was convinced that disciples of Christ are given the authority to cast out oppression from the life of the community. The real unclean spirits to be opposed by Christians are racism, sexism, and classism, which act in concert to give us the ghetto and human brokenness.

The Church of All Nations was experiencing a renewal of faith. The local community challenged it to reformulate the themes of faith in accordance with the social reality of the Latino poor. A list of social concerns was drawn up to further concretize the first goal of the project. Some of the fundamentalists in the church wished to keep the discussion focused on matters of liturgy and worship. They did not want to address the social, political, economic, and cultural questions that cried out for attention. After much discussion and debate, a decision was made to link prayer, Bible study, and social concerns together in order to examine the relationship between faith and the community.

A series of educational forums was planned and fliers were distributed to the community, inviting people to attend. The forums addressed four areas: immigrants' rights, drug abuse, housing justice, and teenage pregnancy. They were helpful in raising the level of awareness about racism, sexism, and classism. The church selected several films to which the community was also invited: *El Norte,* examining the plight of an undocumented brother and sister fleeing military repression in Guatemala;[1] *La Operación,* studying the United States' policy of sterilization implemented in Puerto Rico in the late 1940s and 1950s;[2] *Puerto Rico: Paradise Invaded,* exploring the impact of neocolonialism in Puerto Rican society;[3] *The Heart of the Lower East Side,* looking at housing rights issues in lower Manhattan;[4] and *The Cross and the Switchblade,* describing evangelist Dave Wilkerson's work with New York City gangs.[5]

The films played a critical role in laying a foundation for developing tools of critical analysis. The issues raised by the films were related to the educational forums and Bible study. A significant shift in perception was caused by the viewing of the film *La Operación.* In the 1940s and 1950s, Puerto Rico's economic structure was undergoing major reconstruction, moving away from agriculture toward industrialization. The new economic structure caused a decline in available jobs and an increase in social misery.[6] Overpopulation on the island was being blamed at the time for the growing level of displacement of Puerto Ricans from the economy. The U.S. government devised a plan to address the problems on the island by encouraging not only migration to the States but also sterilization for women.[7] Many of the women in the church had undergone sterilization because U.S. government planners had convinced them it was an act of patriotism toward Puerto Rico. Moreover, they were told by medical officials that it was possible to reverse the operation.

According to the film *La Operación,* one out of every three women were sterilized in the 1940s and 1950s in Puerto Rico. The film alleged that the goal of the so-called "population control" policy was to bring about zero population growth by sterilizing all Puerto Rican women of childbearing age. Carmen stood up after viewing the film and said, "I was one of those women sterilized. I got the operation. We were deceived by the government. It was an injustice to us all." One of the men present also spoke: "That policy of sterilization was in reality a policy to exterminate the Puerto Rican people. We are just a colony of the United States." He never missed a film, forum, or Bible study after that. The film related to all the complex issues inherent in the dynamics of racism, classism, and sexism. It was especially helpful in providing people with an analytic framework for looking at issues.

The social-witness dimensions of scripture were rediscovered with the aid of the films and educational forums. Tracing the special status given the poor and oppressed in scripture emerged as a fresh new way of interpreting the Bible. Faith was breaking out of its private shell and into the world to face its problems. A subgroup of the congregation was established that adopted the name of Grupo Shalom (Shalom group). It functioned as a base community through which social action dimensions of the church's ministry could be developed. Shalom was chosen as the name of the group because it describes the story of God's redemptive action in history: the establishment of peace through communal right relationships.

The Center for Immigrants' Rights conducted an educational forum that included a viewing of the film *El Norte* and a workshop. One section of the workshop was attended by the Latin American Caucus of the New York Annual Conference of the United Methodist Church. CIR sharpened even more our conceptual tools for looking at the dynamics behind Latino marginalization and oppression. Persons were introduced to basic paralegal skills so they might better serve the growing undocumented Latino population. CIR enabled the members of the Church of All Nations to reread the situation in Central America through refugee eyes.

The issues of racism, classism, and sexism reached a dramatic peak for the congregation in regard to one case. A young Guatemalan refugee family was discovered sleeping in the back seat of a car parked in the lot of one of the upstate churches of the New York Annual Conference. Carlos and Maria had come to the United States fleeing the reign of murder, torture, and terror in their country and hoping to find a safe haven here. The couple had received help and support from many individual ministers and newly made friends over the months since they arrived illegally in the country; however, their lack of legal status left them in a vulnerable position. The Church of All Nations and CIR's staff lawyer were called to discuss the possibility of either labor certification or political asylum for the couple. When we received the telephone call about Carlos and Maria's situation, their undocumented status had already become a conference issue.

The church knew it would be difficult to acquire labor certification, but getting political asylum would be even more unlikely. CIR had trained members of the church well in basic immigration law. They knew that less than 2 percent of all Central Americans who petition for political asylum ever receive it; hence, the legal route would be very difficult. For the U.S. government to grant political asylum to citizens of Guatemala would be equivalent to admitting error in its policy in Central America. The massive extent of human brutalization there is the result of over $10 billion in military aid that the Reagan administration has funneled into the region. The total number of police and armed forces in Central America more than doubled between 1978 and 1987.[8]

The New York Annual Conference adopted resolutions at its annual meeting supporting the Sanctuary movement, the defense of the rights of refugees and immigrants, and an end to war in Central America. The crucified Christ came before the New York Annual Conference in the form of a young Guatemalan family, but key leaders of the conference could not decide what course of action to take. Maria was even pregnant at the time, which emphasized the need for some positive measures to be taken very soon. The conference had allowed Carlos and Maria to stay at one of its camps; meanwhile, a number of ministers were helping the couple with gifts of money and Carlos was being employed at the camp and paid out of a discretionary fund. One pastor had committed himself to

see the family through the delivery of the baby, at consid-
erable personal expense. In addition to questions about
acquiring legal documentation to be in the country, the
conference leadership struggled over whether Carlos
should be employed at the church camp, since he was an
undocumented person. Some of the key leaders argued
that his employment would create too much controversy
within the Annual Conference. It would look bad if the
conference broke the law. The plight of the Guatemalan
couple was forgotten in the discussion about employabil-
ity, which centered largely around the conference's
image. Jesus repeatedly broke the Sabbath laws and various social conventions in order to respond to human suffering, but influential leadership in the conference was not
about to act in behalf of the oppressed.

Carlos and Maria's fate was debated in a boardroom
secure from the horrors of war. The lawyer reassured conference leaders that a moral option favoring the couple
would not legally endanger the conference. The new immigration bill that carried heavy employer penalties had
not yet been passed.[9] The real justice issue was not the
question of the legality of Carlos's employment; rather, it
had to do with the U.S. government's narrow interpretation of the Geneva Convention (1949), the United Nations
Protocol (1967), and the Refugee Act (1980), which did not
recognize the legitimate claims of Central American refugees to receive safe haven.

Carlos and Maria lost hope in the conference. After
Maria gave birth to a beautiful girl, they thanked the individuals who had helped them and left the State of New
York. We have not heard a word from them since they left.
The conference's image was saved from any blemish, and
some of the staff did not have to deal with the controversy
that would have come. The conference was given an opportunity to declare sanctuary, to bear witness to the special option for the poor, and to invite Christ into its
presence, but it chose merely to allow Carlos and Maria to
stay at the camp. In the end only the status quo really
benefited from the way the situation was handled. The

Church of All Nations was left to draw its own conclusion: namely, that poor Guatemalan peasants are not as important as the status quo to the North American church hierarchy. Members of the church felt the big mistake was seeking help from the conference. The situation should have been handled exclusively at the local level.

The treatment the Guatemalan couple received at the hands of the New York Annual Conference deeply affected me. Guatemala is my father's country. The story of human suffering that the couple shared caused me to recollect stories my father told me about his youth. Father worked on a United Fruit Company plantation in Guatemala for stretches of up to sixteen hours long. He recalled that workers were paid less than a dollar a day for their labor. At the time, the United States was backing the government of President Jorge Ubico, insisting that Guatemala was on the road to democracy under his leadership. However, Ubico was no more than a vicious dictator who was slaughtering his own people. My father participated in the revolution of 1944 that overthrew Ubico. He was not a communist revolutionary but a campesino worker filled with a vision of a more just society. Indeed, the reformist government of Jacobo Arbenz—which continued to build on the foundation established by Juan José Arévalo, the successor to Ubico—could be characterized as a liberal capitalist democracy.[10]

Jacobo Arbenz's government was overthrown with CIA help in 1954. Father fled Guatemala, made his way through a couple of Central American countries, and eventually came to the United States, where he married the Puerto Rican woman who became my mother. He became a United States citizen, but never lived in the States for any long period of time. He devoted all of his adult life to the ocean as a merchant seaman. Now that he has retired from the merchant marine, he lives in a village in South America, together with his new wife and two sons, and keeps busy by running a small bread bakery. Guatemala will never again feel like home to him. Exile has become a way of life.

The incident with Carlos and Maria caused me to wonder about the church's claim to exist for the oppressed. I wondered if the North American church could be truly transformed by the people unless there was also a change in the posture of its leadership.

Goal Two: To stimulate the development of leadership for the purpose of empowerment of the local Latino community. Members of the church were asked to keep journals and take responsibility for aspects of the project as an initial step toward actualizing this second goal. Volunteers were delegated the job of distributing flyers throughout the community and inviting people from the Lower East Side to participate in the workshops, films, and Bible study.

Two persons emerged as crucial for the development of the project and its focus of linking faith to social action. Jessica and Hector were given responsibility for major aspects of the church's social-witness project. They took charge of the Bible study and used secondary sources of biblical interpretation to give shape to the sessions. They read regularly from such journals as *Sojourners* to broaden their traditional faith perspective by reference to a strong social-witness position. Because the films and forums were organized to interact with the content of the Bible study, Jessica and Hector were able to arrive at a new way of interpreting scripture that allowed the social context to address the Bible with its questions. The teaching method they employed as study facilitators was dialogical and participatory. One of the Bible study participants, Carmen, strongly opposed such a method for conducting a study session because she felt only experts could really teach, not lay persons. Her mind was changed during one of the dialogical study sessions when the group was discussing the Magnificat (Luke 1:46–55). Carmen observed that in this passage Mary was describing the special relationship that God has with the poor and with women. She pointed out how the poor are exalted and the rich are sent away empty. The signs of the new age were initially revealed to the world through Elizabeth and Mary. Carmen spoke with amazement in her voice because she recognized that God had chosen two women as instruments of divine revelation.

The Bible study was crucial for the development of leadership. In one session the group turned its attention to Ezekiel 37. The text helped to sharpen the meaning of community empowerment for those attending the Bible study that day. The metaphor of the valley of dry bones was related to that form of church life which has separated from or escaped reality—the *domingero* church, the one-hour-a-week church. Jessica had picked the text and led the discussion, which focused on the Spirit of Yahweh. Ezekiel 37 indicates that the Spirit is a source of empowerment and renewal for a people in despair; indeed, the renewal of the people of Judah and their spiritual awakening was made possible because of Ezekiel's prophetic preaching. The congregation was able to interpret the role of the church in terms of the image of renewal offered to it by Ezekiel 37, with its call for prophetic words and deeds. It connected the text to the idea of community as wholeness and inclusiveness.

In the course of the Bible study the message of the Christian Right, which is broadcast regularly over Spanish-speaking television stations, was compared to Ezekiel's prophetic word. The language of the television evangelist is very appealing to many Latino church members. The right-wing political philosophy often escapes detection when embedded in the Christian language that is used. Carmen was once a strict evangelical and literalist, but she was shifting her perspective as a result of participation in the Bible study. She raised questions about the spiritual agenda of the Christian Right. She compared the message of the television evangelists to the message she had been finding in Ezekiel 37. She concluded that many of the southern-based Christian broadcast evangelists were actually preaching a doctrine of exclusion and white supremacy. Chapter 37 of Ezekiel made it clear to Carmen that God's Spirit renews and reunites the community around the ideals of the Mosaic covenant. The Christian Right's preaching masked a social agenda based on the politics of oppression. Carmen could no longer blindly accept the hidden agenda of the television evangelists. She understood prophetic preaching to mean that God brings the politics of justice to bear on the life of the whole community. Her opinion was shared by most of the participants in the Bible study.

A cadre of leaders emerged within the congregation empowered by the reading and sharing of scripture. The idea of God's option for the poor and oppressed inspired a new level of biblical insight and a desire for relating to the larger Latino poor community. Most of the members of the church are themselves very poor, and thus the discovery of God's special relationship to them was a source of real empowerment and transformation. Persons were expressing their sense of commitment by hosting workshops, in addition to allowing outside social action groups to use the church's space for meeting. Even a formerly inactive youth group felt transformed by the Spirit. The group presented a workshop for the church and members of the local community on the issue of teenage pregnancy. The presentation was made with incredible sensitivity, and even some of the more conservative older members learned to see the question from the teenagers' point of view. The local church thus helped empower the larger community by making available both church space and human resources.

Goal Three: To increase the interaction between the congregation and the community. The design of the project ensured that the Bible study would interact with the workshops and educational forums. This design led to a new understanding of scripture, a sense of empowerment in the local church, and a commitment to relate the church to the local community. The congregation made the church space available to a number of social justice groups as a sign of its intention of realizing the third goal. The building was used by local housing groups, a national immigrants' rights coalition, a city-wide coalition made up of organizations advocating the rights of undocumented women, and such international groups as Filipinos Against the Marcos Dictatorship (the group backed Corazon Aquino) and a Salvadoran refugee rights group.

The Center for Immigrants' Rights used the church social hall to make numerous presentations to the local community about the plight of Guatemalan and Salvadoran refugees and the war in Central America. Space was also donated to this organization so it could offer paralegal training in immigration law to persons from church agencies, union representatives from the International Ladies' Garment Workers' Union (ILGWU), social workers, and representatives from housing organizations. Members of the church were strongly urged to attend the organization meetings to develop greater sensitivity to justice issues through personal contact. Five members of the Church of All Nations enrolled in a paralegal workshop. Jessica even did some volunteer work for CIR and translated literature into Spanish. The church enabled CIR to cosponsor a public forum together with a local peace organization that was dedicated to the study of the impact of militarism on the poor in the Third World and the United States.

Goal Four: To embrace one or two specific areas for social action. The social action issues to which the congregation decided to commit itself centered on justice advocacy for Central American refugees and the housing rights of the homeless. In the area of immigrants' rights, the church took an active part in preparing for a major public event held on the National Day of Justice in 1985 entitled "The New York Public Hearing on the Plight of the Undocumented Immigrants and Refugees in New York City." The purpose of the event was to place before the public eye the extremely oppressive situation faced by undocumented immigrants. Testimony was given by immigrant and refugee communities, as well as by legal, academic, church, and a host of other immigrants' rights groups. The testimony was presented to a panel of New York's elected officials and religious leaders.[11]

When the congregation became involved in a housing rights issue on behalf of seventy-two homesteading families, we helped them organize a housing coalition, which met regularly in the church building. We also contacted the Center for Constitutional Rights (CCR) in order to find legal representation for those families facing eviction from city-owned buildings. (I remember meeting Arthur Kinoy while riding the elevator up to the CCR's conference room. Mr. Kinoy has been one of the key attorneys of the civil rights movement since 1960. He teaches constitutional law at Rutgers University Law School and is vice-president of CCR and a leader of the National Lawyers Guild. He was the main speaker at the public hearings on the plight of the undocumented in New York City.) Representatives of the families handed the CCR lawyers a folder full of documents telling the history of relations between the city agency that manages municipal property, the Department of Housing Preservation and Development, and the homesteading families. The lawyers reviewed the documents over a period of two weeks and determined that the families had a very good chance of stopping the eviction and receiving title to the property as promised by the city. CCR handled the case at no cost to the families.

The church's involvement in the issue went further than making contact with the lawyers. A public demonstration to be held at City Hall was organized through the newly formed housing coalition, which adopted the name "Valentine Day Committee for Housing Justice." (The scheduled demonstration happened to fall on Valentine's Day.) Regular mailings about the demonstration went out to housing organizations and churches across the city, calling for their support in protesting the housing-for-profit system. The committee's demands included the following:

Amnesty for all people presently occupying and re-storing city properties. Evictions and harassment of families and individuals must be ended.

No sales of city-owned buildings to private develop-ers. Community proposals must have priority and must serve as the basis for development.

Quicker transfer of ownership to low- and moderate-income tenants and self-help rehab groups. No more red tape through arbitrary and selective enforcement of codes.

Maintain tenant buildings, safe and habitable, as any other responsible landlord should under the law.

Stop warehousing people in shelters and hotels. Stop the proliferation of empty apartments and buildings.

These demands were given full coverage in the Spanish-language television news coverage of the demonstration.

The homesteading families' case was in court for three years, but they won the right to enter an official home-steading program: that is to say, a city-sponsored tene-ment rehabilitation program leading to ownership. The renewal process started by the congregation and given shape through this project resulted in concrete commu-nity action on behalf of the "least among us." The gospel was allowed its power of transformation as soon as the special option for the poor and oppressed was made credi-ble to the worshiping community. The middle-class church can also experience transformation through a simi-lar intentional process of growth in faith and action.

MAMI

nobody ever looks to your
street where the buildings
fall, alone with the junkies

that use the rooftops,
needles still dangling
from arms and Spanglish commentary

all the way down. uptown
they will never mention Boricua
mothers with faces that tell of

another age and hands only slaves
would recognize. nobody on the other
side of the world that turns its head

this way to spit would think to call
these women Mami. . . .

5

Personal Renewal

Many people thought the Church of All Nations was a place to get away from the frustrations of daily life. They believed spirituality had nothing to do with the dynamics of racism, classism, and sexism. In their eyes, the pulpit was not to be used to promote an understanding of social, political, economic, and cultural problems. Prayer and the devotional life were the marks of true discipleship. The effort to raise the theological and social-ethical awareness of the church led to the use of an action/reflection approach something like that used in Latin America.

There the poor gather in small reflection groups, called basic Christian communities or Christian base communities, to discuss scripture and to discover how the Bible relates to all aspects of their lives. They come to understand how the gospel penetrates every area of social existence, affirms the most wretched members of society, and empowers the most despised classes to work for the creation of a more just human social order. Through the process of biblical reflection and increased social awareness, the poor of the Christian base communities are overcoming the internal scars of oppression that had convinced them of their own powerlessness. These communities are challenging the oppressive social order in Latin America by calling for a reformation of society based on the exercise of power from the bottom up. The new society envisioned by these Christian base communities in Latin America will not be hierarchically organized; it will be organized around the concern for mutual empowerment.[1]

The Christian base communities of Latin America engage in social action projects at the grass-roots level at great risk to personal life. The growth of these communities represents a mass movement for social reform that has no parallel in the Latino community in the United States. The developing Christian base community in the Church of All Nations focused upon creating positive change at the local community level. Racial and economic justice as well as community organization for fair housing were the focus of the social-witness activities of the emerging group. Those participating in the groups learned how faith can reach into those places of community life that are in need of transformation. Josefa, Lydia, Jessica, Miriam, and Carmen are examples of persons in the church who were struggling to overcome a private faith tradition and to redefine spirituality as social engagement.

Josefa

Josefa experienced a change in perception that made her more sensitive to the causes of poverty and oppression. Although Josefa is not a member of the middle class by North American standards, she shares the North American middle-class value system. Josefa's style of living is considerably better than most of the Latino poor community. For years, she has traveled from New York City to a family home in Puerto Rico for the winter months. The work ethic implanted by Protestant missionaries in Josefa's mind motivated her to save and buy a modest home on the island. Regrettably, that work ethic produced a high level of intolerance for the poor and a strong identification with the better off. She was convinced that Puerto Ricans were the primary cause of the existence of slums such as the South Bronx and the Lower East Side. Her perceptions told her that neighborhoods turn into ghettos when Puerto Ricans move into them. Josefa never hesitated to share these perceptions with the congregation.

Josefa's insensitivity toward the working Puerto Rican poor of the Lower East Side was often a source of tension within the church. Many members of the congregation live in the heart of the ghetto. They are hardworking people, but they never seem to improve their social and economic status. The poor could certainly tell Josefa that the wretched living conditions characteristic of the community are not caused by Puerto Ricans. The congregation was not sure how to deal with Josefa's mean-spirited notions about what causes the existence of the ghetto.

Josefa's husband enjoyed a much warmer relationship to members of the church. He did not share his wife's perceptions about the ghetto. Eddie had daily contact with the working Puerto Rican poor through his job as superintendent of a series of tenement buildings. The struggle of the community was always present to him in the faces of the young men and women who passed him each day on their way to buy dope. That waste of life caused Eddie a great deal of pain. Eddie moved about the neighborhood. He spent part of his time listening to other people's stories of painful attempts to make ends meet on minimum wages. The church was not a major part of Eddie's life during his formative years in Puerto Rico. The unchurched working poor have always been his main source of information.

Eddie maintained a very low profile in the church. However, he was not reluctant to talk compassionately of the plight of the Puerto Rican poor. Members of the church always looked forward to the news Eddie would bring back from Puerto Rico following his winter vacations at the family home. He always made a point of talking about the level of despair in Puerto Rico. He would describe how poverty assaults the senses. He never blamed the Puerto Rican people for their conditions of life. Eddie saw a connection between the misery of the ghetto and the despair in Puerto Rican hamlets. Eddie would always ask the members of the church to pray for the Puerto Ricans in the barrio and on the island.

Josefa worked very hard all her life. She overcame the poverty of her childhood through hard work and self-discipline. She believed her success also included the right to condemn the chronically unemployed young men standing on so many street corners of the Lower East Side. Josefa felt that people are poor due to laziness or bad moral character. The prevailing social wisdom did not contradict her basic assumptions about social reality. Moreover, her immediate living context seemed to reinforce her perceptions as well. Josefa lived in a six-story building that had gone co-op. Luckily, her apartment was protected by rent-control laws, and this enabled her to enjoy the benefits of neighborhood revitalization, sometimes called gentrification. But she failed to see that her quality of life had improved because of the displacement of the poor by the middle class through this process.

My interviews with her give some insight into how her particular worldview underwent change.

INTERVIEW 1: JOSEFA

PASTOR: Josefa, what is your background?

JOSEFA: Well, I came here very young from Puerto Rico. I was married here, had my children here, and have been around for some thirty-five years. Thanks be to God, all has been real good!

PASTOR: What part of Puerto Rico do you call home? How is life in the United States?

JOSEFA: I come from Lajas. Compared to Puerto Rico, work is much better in the United States because one can make a living here. Over there, life was becoming very difficult for me. I came at an early age because I wanted to progress. Thanks to God, I was here a few years; then I went back to Puerto Rico and stayed four months. I could not find work. I had to return to the United States to find work.

PASTOR: When did you leave Puerto Rico? How was life at that time?

JOSEFA: I left in 1948. At that time, life was very inexpensive and one lived well on what one earned. For some reason they started to close the sewing factories. I used to make gloves, but that industry was declining. This forced me to look for a new way to make a dollar, and I came to the United States. In 1950, I returned to stay, but there was no work and again I came to the States. Then, I met my husband, and we have struggled together since then. I had all my children here.

PASTOR: Did many Puerto Ricans come to the United States in 1948?

JOSEFA: In 1948, not many were coming to the States. I was the second person to leave my barrio. After 1951, people really started coming to the States. There was no work on the island.

PASTOR: How was the Lower East Side of Manhattan when you first arrived?

JOSEFA: Well, I did not live in this area then. I lived uptown on 103rd Street. It was a good neighborhood. You could go out alone at night and nobody seemed to bother you. It wasn't like it is today. The barrio had all kinds of Latinos, Blacks, and Jews. I moved to Delancey Street in 1952.

PASTOR: How do you see life in the States for a Latina woman?

JOSEFA: We make life what it is. If one raises children under the guidance of God, even when the children stop going to church, they will always have the fear of God within them. I have always reminded them of the existence of God. They have been well raised. We were poor, but we gave them what we could. Thanks to God, they have worked and progressed. I don't know what it would be like to raise children today. Everything is changing with the passing years.

PASTOR: What do you think the political future of Puerto Rico will be, independence, commonwealth, or statehood?

JOSEFA: I left Puerto Rico many years ago, but I believe the people who live on the island all year round should decide their future. They know what is best for their lives. Personally, I hope it remains as it is because, for better or worse, people live and share what

they have, despite the fact there are too many for-
eigners. We can't decide what will happen.

PASTOR: How do you understand the role of the church
in the world?

JOSEFA: Well, the church is delivering a spiritual message to the world. There are people that don't hear
the Word; but in Puerto Rico, God's Word is being
preached everywhere. The deaf refuse to hear.

PASTOR: What is the church's theme?

JOSEFA: Well, that one day the Lord is coming and who-
ever is not prepared will be left behind. Meanwhile,
we must help people. The poor must be allowed to
live and the thirsty must be given to drink.

PASTOR: Is there any evidence that the church is involved in the life of the poor?

JOSEFA: Yes, there is evidence. We are doing it right
here in our church.

PASTOR: You mentioned that the church must stay
clear of politics, but take the case of South Africa.
Blacks have no rights. They are not considered citizens and own no property. The government op-
presses them cruelly. What is the role of the church
in such a situation?

JOSEFA: The church has to defend the oppressed. We
can't be in favor of this situation because we are Christians.

Josefa's involvement in the action/reflection project
helped to change her perceptions of the causes of poverty
and oppression. She discovered that her God-talk loses all
credibility if it lacks authentic struggle with the dynamics
implicit in social reality. Through a process of intentional
biblical, social, and personal reflection Josefa learned to
see the world from the perspective of despised humanity.
The Word of God began to pose new questions for her
faith, and the old missionary theology gave way to the God
who takes sides with the oppressed. At first, Josefa's
change in consciousness came slowly and sporadically. She
began to reconsider her interpretation of the reasons for

the existence of the ghetto. Eventually, she was able to understand how racism and economic injustice are responsible for creating ghettos and marginalizing Puerto Ricans. Josefa started to raise questions about her social environment she had never considered in the past. "In Puerto Rico people did not live so badly. Why do we live this way here? Why are the poor being pushed out?"

One fall evening, Josefa shared a perception about the streets that indicated a move to new levels of interpretation. Normally, Josefa would look around at the abandoned tenements and the mounds of garbage piled on the streets disapprovingly and blame the poor. On this particular night, Josefa surprised everyone by taking a different line of reasoning regarding the condition of the neighborhood. She blamed the biggest slumlord on the Lower East Side—city government. Josefa had shifted the blame from the personal to the social and structural levels. Clearly, this indicated that Josefa was attempting to understand the slum in light of much larger systemic factors. Her comments indicated that she was reidentifying with the voiceless and powerless people of the ghetto. A second interview illustrates these changes.

INTERVIEW 2: JOSEFA

PASTOR: Josefa, would you talk about the various aspects of our action/reflection project, indicating how it has helped you to understand the relationship between faith and social witness?

JOSEFA: I have been able to understand what it means to be a church in the community. First, we must help others to be able to say, "We are Christians." The church is a part of the world. I would say the various study events have a great deal of importance for the life of the church. I hope more people participate in them. The films have been very good and instructive. They taught me a great deal.

PASTOR: Can you give an example of how the films have helped you?

JOSEFA: Well, in this country if we don't read the newspapers and make an effort to become informed, we simply think that refugees or immigrants have it easy. The undocumented have problems like us, but they are mistreated. The newspapers describe how the undocumented work more hours, earn less money, and are treated differently from citizens. They are not treated like human beings. I believe we all have the same rights and should be treated justly. Everyone should be equal. The films and workshops have helped me to see this situation.

PASTOR: You talked about the undocumented. What can you say about what is happening in our community?

JOSEFA: Well, I understand that everyone should seek God. For instance, they should come to this church where we struggle so that things might change in the community. Things don't work justly in our society.

PASTOR: Are there elements of racism, classism, and sexism at work in the community or in the treatment of undocumented persons?

JOSEFA: Yes, there certainly are. Just read the papers! God tells us that we are all his children. I believe those who discriminate need God in their hearts. God came to save us all.

PASTOR: What are the landlords searching for on the Lower East Side?

JOSEFA: The landlords are looking to make money, nothing else. It doesn't bother them to see someone living under a bridge or in the park. This means nothing to them. They have no compassion for the homeless. Christ is not in their hearts.

PASTOR: How has the Bible study helped you to see things anew?

JOSEFA: The Bible study has taught me to care more for humanity. I have learned to see things differently. One new perspective I remember came when we studied John the Baptist talking about repentance. He accused officials of defrauding the people. Christ was not in the hearts of the officials. Sharing what we have is true repentance. We must treat everyone like we would treat ourselves.

PASTOR: What is the significance of God's self-revelation to Mary and Elizabeth?

JOSEFA: God is teaching us that we must show humility and give what we have. God looked for Mary, a poor child, to teach us humility. Jesus was the greatest man, but he was born in a stable. God didn't choose a palace, but a stable!

PASTOR: What kind of message is God giving to the wealthy in all of this?

JOSEFA: They shouldn't take everything, because everything belongs to God. The rich idolize money, instead of putting God first. We should share what we have with those who have nothing.

One of the films, *Puerto Rico: Paradise Invaded*, enabled Josefa to deal with a dimension of colonial history she had never considered. The missionary legacy had convinced Josefa that all Puerto Ricans on the island experienced reality like the middle class. The film helped Josefa come to terms with the process of the dispossession of Puerto Ricans from the land and their eventual forced migration to the United States, owing to the restructured colonial economy. Some of the language in the film was revolutionary, but it did not prevent Josefa from accepting the film's assumptions about the colonial relationship between the United States and Puerto Rico. The analytic framework of the film gave Josefa a basis for looking at the connection between colonialism on the island and Puerto Rican poverty and oppression.

Josefa sought to improve her relationships with the congregation. She accepted more responsibility for church-related functions. She no longer perceived the Lower East Side in traditional middle-class categories. She searched for the social factors implicit in the community's problems; indeed, Josefa started to monitor the community board's policy on local housing and economic justice issues. Soon Josefa was sharing her experience with the congregation concerning racist attacks on her family at her largely gentrified building. Her family was being blamed when something was found broken in the building. Josefa got involved in a union-sponsored activity that took her to Washington, D.C., to participate in a demonstration march for peace and jobs. Faith was transformed for her as she began to see the life of the community in light of the meaning of the church.

Lydia

Lydia was nurtured in a very rich and traditional Christian evangelical belief system. For her, faith meant hard work, self-control, frugality, and a personal relationship with God. Lydia was convinced that human effort could not alter the course of history. The action/reflection project helped to enlarge Lydia's belief system, enabling her to include responsible Christian action within her faith system. She learned to value social action as one part of God's plan for human transformation. Social witness is part of the mission of the church. Lydia discovered the Jesus who overturned the tables of the money changers at the Temple in Jerusalem. She came to the realization that the church is called by God to be an interpreter of the times, an advocate of the poor, an irritant to the status quo, and a visionary for transformation.

Lydia's roots go back to a small village in Puerto Rico. Her family was poor but had great spiritual resources. Lydia came to the United States with her husband in the hope of finding a better way of life. She lived on the top floor of a five-story walk-up. That apartment has been home to her for the last thirty years. Lydia's first impressions of city life came through the kitchen window, which overlooks the rooftops of adjoining tenements. The imprint left by that view was the image of a dirty city. Lydia has always considered the church to be a place of refuge and cultural self-expression. The church is the one place in the community that provides sanctuary from an alienating urban cultural experience. Churches are not like dirty rooftops seen from kitchen windows.

The early years of life in the States seemed full of promise for Lydia and her husband. The family saved enough money to start a dry cleaning business, everyone was adjusting to city life, and the neighborhood was treating them in a friendly way. Lydia attended a church that made her feel at home, although her husband refused to go with her, out of his conviction that organized religion is hypocrisy. Within a few years, Lydia's life would go into a downward spiral. Her husband developed a drinking habit, started seeing other women, and lost the family business. Lydia stood faithfully at her husband's side during the difficult years that followed. She was able to forgive her husband during the years of personal crisis. The church helped to sustain Lydia during the worst period of the turbulent years. Lydia's faith deepened because she felt God would see her through the pain.

Just before the start of the action/reflection project Lydia experienced the death of a son. The shock caused her to withdraw emotionally from the life of the church. Other members of the church did not believe Lydia would want to become involved in the project. But Lydia was invited to take an active role, and much to everyone's surprise she accepted the invitation. She was delighted about being asked to give her opinion on religious matters. It meant a great deal to Lydia that she was being taken seriously, despite never having received a formal education. Lydia believed that God was calling her to participate in the project as a way out of the painful solitude into which the death of her son had thrown her.

The Church of All Nations may never know a more loving and authentically faithful woman than Lydia. She never blamed the victims of human injustice. Lydia interpreted the suffering of the Latino poor of the Lower East Side as a sign of human indifference. An old Talmudic saying captures the spirit of Lydia: "Judge not the poor for their poverty, but rather judge the community for its indifference." Lydia did not have the vocabulary necessary to describe the causes of poverty, oppression, and human suffering, yet she was convinced that these realities depend upon much larger issues than mere individuals. Lydia believed the poor were in need of God's love and salvation, perhaps more than the well off. The poor know the suffering of Jesus better than the rich. She became involved in the project, and one Sunday she presented the congregation with a prayer for the service. Her kindness comes through in her prayer:

> Beloved Lord and Father, I give you thanks for your loving kindness. Be with us and watch over us. Fill us with your Holy Spirit. Watch over our loved ones. Grant them health and be with the sick. Now, Lord, I pray for the Lower East Side. You know how our brothers and sisters are living with so many problems. They are struggling to have a home, and the government does so little to help. You know the situation of the homeless. Be with them and teach us to see them as human beings who suffer like we do. This I ask in the name of Jesus Christ. Amen.

Lydia's sense of faith kept her strongly identified with the experience of the very poor. She would eventually develop a better understanding of the causes behind poverty. The first interview reveals Lydia's sense of fairness and provides some insight into her change process.

INTERVIEW 1: LYDIA

PASTOR: What village are you from in Puerto Rico?

LYDIA: I come from Yauco, the coffee village. I have been in New York City for twenty-nine years. I like it. I have my family here, my children.

PASTOR: What made you come to the States?

LYDIA: Well, my husband came first. Later, after he found work, he sent for us. At first, life here was difficult. One had to learn how to get around the city. But I learned.

PASTOR: Can you describe your first impression of life in the States?

LYDIA: My very first impression of New York? I said, "Look how dirty the rooftops are!" It's ugly, too many stairs. I am used to it here now and I would not like to return to Puerto Rico, especially with all that is happening over there.

PASTOR: How was this area of New York then?

LYDIA: Life was easygoing in the area. We weren't afraid. You could shop with very little money. Things were cheap. Today, everything is more difficult. I think things are this way because of a depression and the system of government.

PASTOR: When did you start coming to church?

LYDIA: I started coming to this church after being here for around four years. My friend invited me to come. When I first got here, I didn't attend church. I didn't really attend church in Puerto Rico. Here I visited a Catholic church on Twelfth Street, but I didn't like the atmosphere. There wasn't any sense of community. Everyone went their own way. So, I stayed home until my friend invited me to attend church. I stayed. I found a community. I could talk to people.

PASTOR: How would you describe the theology of the services?

LYDIA: The last pastor talked about relationships with God and one another.

PASTOR: How do you see the changes in this area?

LYDIA: The changes are not favorable to the poor. The system favors the rich, the "Americans." The poor are being pushed to the margins. We need to progress.

PASTOR: What is the relationship between faith and the community?

LYDIA: Faith relates to the world in terms of prayer, love, and sharing. I think this is all. Tell people, "God loves you."

PASTOR: What would you say if someone asked, "What is salvation?"

LYDIA: I would say that salvation is Jesus Christ! He came to save us.

One of the films viewed at the church as a part of the project, *La Operación,* put Lydia in touch with some deep unconscious wounds. The federal government of the United States had implemented a program of sterilization in Puerto Rico in the 1950s. Sterilization was introduced on the island ostensibly to control the problem of population. Social stresses within Puerto Rican society were not blamed on the colonial economic structure; instead, surplus population was identified as the major contributing factor to impoverishment on the island. (See chapter 4.)

As Lydia viewed the film she became increasingly convinced that the purpose of the sterilization policy was to achieve 100 percent sterilization for Puerto Rican women of childbearing age. The demonic intentions of the federal government program, as shown in the film, outraged Lydia. She had undergone the operation in the belief that she was doing something important for Puerto Rican society. Now she understood that the policy had an evil intent, the potential genocide of the Puerto Rican people. When one of the doctors who helped implement the program in Puerto Rico was found practicing medicine at Lincoln Hospital in the South Bronx, the local Puerto Rican community demonstrated and had him removed. Her opinion of the government shifted significantly from one of trust to one of suspicion.

INTERVIEW 2: LYDIA

PASTOR: We have talked about the relationship between faith and the community for some months. Can you tell me something about this relationship?

LYDIA: Well, faith and community are related in one single place, the church. I have liked the films. They have exposed me to many things which we may have ignored. I have given of myself in the project.

PASTOR: Would you say something about the films? You

say they have exposed you to new things. What things? How has your understanding changed?

LYDIA: Well, thinking back, I don't think I would have gotten sterilized. I have learned how God works within the community. I see how the Loisaida is, and that there are people who have faith and continue to struggle for what is theirs. I have learned that one cannot wait for things to happen. We have to struggle and make things happen.

PASTOR: We set out to examine the dynamics of racism, classism, and sexism. How do you understand these issues now?

LYDIA: Well, racism can be understood in terms of the landlords who don't want certain races in their buildings. Classism has to do with people who earn less. For instance, people who come from overseas have the juice squeezed out of them because they are paid a misery for a salary. They are unable to progress. The bosses pay good money for people of the same race.

PASTOR: How has the Bible study helped you to examine what is happening in the community?

LYDIA: The Bible study has helped me to understand how things are. There has always been oppression, but the will of God wants things to change. I remember the temptation of Christ by Satan. Christ decided to serve God, not Satan. In this world, people are serving the wrong master.

PASTOR: In the Gospel of Luke, God chooses women to initiate the disclosure of the new covenant at hand. Why?

LYDIA: I think the significance of this is that Maria was poor. She wasn't rich, but poor. This means we shouldn't worship wealth.

PASTOR: What do we need to do to reach the community?

LYDIA: First, we must continue to pray. I think that I can help this community by asking God to help. We need to talk about God's Word. The landlords need to hear God's word. They are selfish!

Jessica

Because the action/reflection project was having definite success in the life of the church, rumors began cir-
culating regarding its content and my politics. One
rumor was that "the pastor has communist tendencies." I
was concerned about the potential threat of the rumors
to the project; hence, I called a number of church members to help in developing a response. One of them was
Jessica.

Jessica said, "I have not heard anything about your having communist tendencies. Most of the people I have
talked to like the project and are getting much out of it.
You know, if by communist tendencies they mean someone who is dissatisfied with the way society is set up, then
I think I have communist tendencies, and so does the
United Methodist Church."

The following Sunday at the worship service, Jessica
confronted the congregation on the issue of the rumor.
Prayers were being written by members of the church on
a regular basis for use in Sunday's liturgy. Jessica used the
following prayer that Sunday:

> Our Father, we come before you in the spirit of praise and
> communion. Allow me to feel the presence of your Holy Spirit
> and Divine Grace. We thank you for all that you have given
> us, for your love. Thank you for the right to call ourselves your
> children. We also give you thanks, O God, for all those persons
> who are working toward world peace and an end to human
> suffering which results from injustice. Lord, you know what
> we are trying to do in this church. Give us your blessing and
> guide us so that we might seek justice in this community. Bless
> us with the gifts necessary for the task. Fill our hearts with love
> for the needy and keep our minds close to you. Grant that we
> might have the unity that is fitting for the body of Christ.
> Amen.

Jessica was a real growth catalyst for the rest of the
congregation. She helped persons experience empowerment and transformation in the Bible study as well as in
the sharing of prayers used in the Sunday service. The

congregation was connecting Bible study, liturgy, and social action into a single focus. The old feeling of powerlessness was lifting like fog from a curving road.

Miriam

Most of the members of the church experienced a degree of transformation by participating in the events offered by the action/reflection model. Miriam underwent a change in her strict evangelical faith posture which understood Christianity in exclusively private terms. She had had a scare with cancer about fifteen years before when the doctors told her she had only six months of life left. The doctors turned out to be wrong in their prognosis. Miriam interpreted her recovery as a miracle. The experience led her to root her faith deeper into the private dimensions of life far from the public domain. Her faith witness was turned into a sharing of the experience of salvation from cancer. She hoped others would "come to the Lord" after hearing her wonderful story of faith.

Miriam's belief system was challenged one afternoon following a workshop on the plight of the undocumented which included testimony from Salvadoran refugees. Her very private level of belief was severely disturbed when she heard of the horrors of war faced by Salvadorans in the name of so-called Christian civilization. She was quite shaken by the refugees' testimony of how men, women, children, and elderly persons were being slaughtered by the military in El Salvador.

Miriam heard about the torture, the rape of women and children, the mutilation of young men, and the brutal murders of infants. The terror characterizing life in El Salvador made the kind of talk she conducted about God appear self-indulgent and senseless. She began to see the face of the crucified Jesus in those of the refugees. The way she understood faith was starting to change because her awareness of human reality and suffering had reached a new level. Miriam began perceiving social reality from a new vantage point based on the interaction of scripture and the world. She appropriated a dimension of the gospel story that had been hidden, which enabled her to see that Jesus walked with social outcasts, persons crushed by oppression, diminished by the state, and rejected by organized religion. The junkie on the street, the corner prostitute, the young high school dropout, the unemployed man hanging out on the corner represented a whole new reality for Miriam. She began to understand how structural factors were behind the problems of the community.

Carmen

Carmen also experienced transformation within her traditional faith posture. The early weeks of the action/reflection project were very threatening for Carmen, although she gained some positive insights during the Bible study, as mentioned in chapter 4. One of the integrating tools that was used in the action/reflection project was the writing of prayers for worship. Carmen was reluctant to participate in this process because she had never finished primary school and felt unable to write. She pulled me aside one morning after the service and shared her fear about writing prayers with me. I agreed to do some editing of the prayers, but told her not to worry about "proper" composition. Carmen is a gifted poet so I encouraged her to forge ahead. Two of the prayers she handed me are reflective of a change process that Carmen experienced through participation in the project. Below is the first prayer:

> Lord and Father, we give you praise, thanks, and honor. You are the God of all things. Owner of creation. You are omnipotent, omnipresent, and full of life. Our lives are your possession and we are surely your instruments. You know our needs. Bless the afflicted. Amen.

This prayer is traditional in its conception of God. Carmen's second prayer reflects a new sense of Christianity as participation in shaping events. Notice the difference:

Heavenly Lord, capable of seeing all things, in whose hands all creation exists, we appeal to your mercy, for this world lacks love for the needy. Illuminate the minds of our national leaders, so that they might see the suffering of the afflicted, particularly the undocumented. The undocumented are in your hands. Permit them to have normal lives. They are human beings of flesh and blood just like the rest of us. It is sad to think of the way the undocumented must live in fear. They fear the authorities as if they were criminals. They left their homeland because of poverty and persecution and are here looking for a better way of life. If justice exists we should dedicate time to finding a solution to this situation. Amen.

Something new has been added to the previous perspective. And the last line of the prayer challenges the church to find a solution to the problem of injustice.

Faith and Justice

The action/reflection base community model enabled the Church of All Nations to play a significant role in the life of the community as a change agent. The Bible study was the cornerstone of the transformation process that had enriched the life of a traditional evangelical church. The church linked faith to justice to act as a change agent in the areas of housing and Central American refugee rights. The gospel was allowed to speak from the underside of history, rather than from the dominant middle-class worldview pervasive in our society. Human action was linked to the notion of God's plan for overcoming oppression, racial discrimination, and economic injustice in society.

Paradoxically, the profound evangelical faith tradition of the congregation was crucial for the development of a genuinely fresh perspective on the Christian tradition. Private faith had already assured members of the church of God's presence in human life at the personal level, but the rereading of scripture from below was now informing them of God's identification with the powerless and voiceless of society. The Church of All Nations learned the

importance of marching to the edges of society to join the
outcasts in their struggle to create more just conditions of
life. Authentic faith was necessary in order to perceive
how God's revelation in history through Jesus Christ takes
place both at the personal and at the social level.

The Church of All Nations recognized that the world's
poor are reclaiming the Christian message. Reading the
scriptures from the perspective of the poor caused a new
level of response to the gospel that introduced a call for
reformation within the local church community. Today's
church leaders are being called to join the struggle of poor
Christians around the world who are leading the way to a
transformed church. Leaders of the church are expected
to reaffirm the transforming dimensions of the gospel, lead
the faithful toward a new understanding of the nature of
the church, and help persons break free of a numbing
status quo. The gospel offers renewal to persons willing to
commit themselves to solidarity with the poor. God promises to bring about a reconciled and transformed creation
out of the justice struggle of the least among us (Matthew
25). In its own limited way, the Church of All Nations
accepted the invitation to walk with the Crucified One in
the local community.

The action/reflection project modified the traditional
faith formulas embodied by members of the church. The
sentimental notion implicit in the formula "Jesus saves"
was given a larger interpretation by applying it to the
social realm. Jesus of Nazareth was rediscovered in terms
of the call to act redemptively as a people of God in the
life of the world. My Latino colleagues were skeptical
about the possibility of helping the North American
Latino church to experience a new dimension of faith. In
their opinion, that church was too conservative, reactionary, and evangelical for renewal. The old-timers claimed
to have attempted everything imaginable to bring about
a new Latino church interested in social witness.

I was not able to accept the hopeless perspective of my
fellow clergy. I was convinced of the possibility for
renewal. Some parts of the North American ecclesial com-

munities were undergoing transformation under the impact of liberation theology and the Sanctuary movement. Why could we not take advantage of the Latin American reality pervasive in the United States and use it to break the isolation of the North American Latino church? Latinos in the United States are learning about the situation of Latin American society through the growing number of Central American refugees taking up residence in the barrio. The civil rights movement headed by Black church leadership is also a part of the thematic universe of the North American Latino church; thus a social-witness tradition was close to home. Finally, the survival concerns of the North American Latino community are finding expression in the church as individuals make personal appeals to God for help. The link between faith and survival is there, although it is seldom experienced as social empowerment from God to create new conditions of life. Nevertheless, the link suggests that the Latino church in the United States could be transformed in the direction so eloquently expressed by poor Christians in Latin America and other parts of the Third World.

The leaders of the church must be willing to undertake a process that will lead to renewal. Local church faith traditions can be respected, but they should also be challenged to become more relevant to the life of society. The cries of the poor are seldom given priority over the complaints of the rich.

The Church of All Nations was capable of listening to the cries of the poor in the local community. Moreover, the church's immersion in the struggles of the poor caused a change in the way scripture was being read and faith experienced. The poor were seen as objects of truth and messengers of transformation. We chose to enter the life of the marginalized, and we experienced their hurt and shared their vision of a just society. As a community called to be the church, we learned to hear the cries of the poor and oppressed that for so long had not been heard in the pews. Our efforts to combine action and reflection rooted discipleship in the struggle of the community.

LATINO TOWN

merengue music is being tapped
rhythmically by tired work feet,
drenching the hot sidewalk in sweat:

it's Latino town and the secondhand
cars, the third and fourth ones too,
are up on jacks being fixed and admired.

it doesn't make a difference on a sábado*
afternoon. it's Latino town and grandmothers
are emerging from the tenements adopting whole

blocks, silently being everyone's abuelita†
it's Latino town and the hydrants are at full force;
scattered cans of Coke and beer are being

gathered by the little children,
who run up to the old man selling piraqua‡
to ask that he open the ends so they can spray

the water at each other, the buses, the
buildings and have a laugh, such a risa.
it's Latino town and at ten o'clock this morning

the Goya little league will begin to play against
Bustelo's little league, and it's beans against café
once again, they say. it's Latino town and Julia

and Tito have opened their first-floor window
real wide listening to the music they put on la
radiola while rehearsing moves for tonight's big

baile.§ it's Latino town and in front of the bodega
sit Don Carlo, Don Pepe, Don Wilfredo, and Charly
on milk boxes emptied of treats, playing dominoes.

it's Latino town, and all the smiles are in
Spanish. . . .

---

*Saturday   ‡snow cone
†granny   §dance

6

The New Reformation:
Solidarity and Connection

The Puerto Rican community in the United States exists
at almost the lowest rung of the economic ladder; Native
Americans occupy the very bottom. Statistics about the
so-called "Hispanic" population tend to mislead the public
about this group. Lumping all persons of Latin American
origin together in a general category labeled Hispanics
distorts the sociological reality and complexity of the Hispanic population in the United States. The Hispanic community in the United States is not socially, economically,
politically, ideologically, or religiously uniform. The special characteristics of each group encompassed by the
term should be considered. Sharpening statistical studies
in this manner will make it possible to grasp reality from
a new vantage point that permits the complex nature of
the Hispanic community to emerge.

"Latino" is the noun most preferred by North American
persons with Latin American cultural roots. Normally, the
term "Hispanic" is not used because it implies an outsider's view of the community deriving from an Anglo
perspective. The term "Latino" reflects the fact that the
Latin American community in the United States is becoming conscious of its history, culture, and political situation
in relation to the dominant society. The Puerto Rican and
the Mexican-American (Chicano) communities represent
two of the largest Latino groups in the United States. The
Church of All Nations serves the Puerto Rican community;
however, the experience of oppression, racial discrimination, economic injustice, invisibility, and sociopolitical

alienation are common to the two largest Latino groups, and to the vast majority of Latinos in the United States as well.

Dehumanization has become a normal experience of daily life for Puerto Ricans living in the ghetto. The infant mortality rate for Puerto Ricans there is higher than that in Honduras. White society almost never takes a close look at the situation of oppression within the Puerto Rican or Latino community. White society has made oppression in the United States synonymous with Black experience. Latinos in the United States have been marginalized from the centers of social and political power as a result of the biracial structure of North American society. The war between North and South in the 1860s, which brought about the end of slavery, deeply imprinted on the U.S. consciousness the image of oppression as perceived through Black/white lenses. In other words, oppression in U.S. society has been understood in terms of the relationships that exist between Black and white society. Why didn't the Mexican-American war imprint the collective mind of white society in such a way that Latino issues might find a hearing in the public domain? The Latino community has remained invisible to North Americans despite the fact that all of the territory from Colorado to California once belonged to Mexico and was occupied by Mexicans and Native Americans. White society has increased its awareness of the wretched conditions pervading the barrios through its work with Central American refugees. Yet, by and large, the Latino experience in the United States continues to be omitted from the language of the progressive North American community. The concern for social justice in Central America has barely been extended into the streets of el barrio.

Latino social reality will continue to be invisible unless the Puerto Rican and Mexican-American communities impact white society. In general, the Latino church in the United States has been partly responsible for the persistent invisibility of its own community by not fully exercising the prophetic role that history has assigned to it. The

Jesus of the unscandalous cross and the Bible of private spirituality have been preached in place of the Jesus who put not only the poor, the outcast, and the sick but also oppressed minorities and women at the heart of his mission.

Latinos in the United States live in subhuman social conditions. The theology emerging from the barrio experience is designed to make sense of the reality of oppression. A Latino theology of survival restores human dignity to a community—be it Puerto Rican, Mexican-American, Dominican, or Central American—stripped of its humanity by a marginalizing social structure. It may appear to the outsider that Latino theology in the United States barrio is strictly otherworldly or compensatory. But barrio theology is much more than otherworldliness. First, the otherworldly dimension of Latino theology coming out of the ghetto experience seeks to describe the transcendent quality of God's kingdom, which is above this world's structures of inequality. God's kingdom points to a new world based on justice and equality. Second, Latino theology in the United States grows out of the experience of racial discrimination and economic marginalization. Survival therefore means altering those dimensions of social reality responsible for Latino dehumanization in the light of God's vision of "other-world-ness." Third, God's promise of a new heaven and a new earth calls into question for Latino theology the present structure of dehumanization and invisibility that marks the existential experience of the ghetto. Fourth, the otherworldliness of Latino theology in the United States context reflects a coded language that seeks to keep alive the barrio's aspirations for social justice.

Toward a New Latino Church in the United States

The Puerto Rican experience illustrates how the otherworldliness of barrio theology is related to the here and now. The Lower East Side's Puerto Rican church community uses otherworldly language to describe the situation of oppression that characterizes the life of the Latino community of the area. God's participation in the life of the community is taken for granted, although the nature of that presence is understood in a very specific way. How does the Puerto Rican church person of the Lower East Side understand God's activity in community life? One might think that the questions to be addressed to the wretched situation of life in the barrio would include the following: "How can God permit us to live in such ruins? How can God stand quietly by and allow so many Puerto Ricans to be pushed out of their apartments, so many children to go hungry, so many young men and women to drop out of school, and so many old people to grow sick without recourse?" Instead, very different questions are asked: "How can God live with us in such ruins? How can God lose apartments with us, go hungry with our children, drop out of school with our young men and women, and grow sick with our old people?" The Puerto Rican faithful realize that God's "otherworldliness" means that the mysterious God of the cross is fully identified with the community's experience of oppression and despair. Otherworldliness means the divine redefinition of what it means to be faithful in this world.

Regrettably, the Latino church has not translated this theological experience into an instrument of empowerment sufficient to impact white society. In this sense, the Latino church differs from the Black church, which has developed powerful institutions over the last two centuries that have sought to reform the morality of white society on the issue of racial justice. The Latino church in the United States must develop a social, economic, and political analysis by which it can link faith to empowerment. Latino Christians in the United States link their faith too often to the conservative Christian Right without thinking of the implications of this alliance for their brothers and sisters in Central America. The Christian Right's use of the symbol system of faith, testimony from persons "helped by God to make it," and references to a so-called "sinless world" easily seduce Latino Christians who are experiencing difficult lives in the barrio.

Latino Christians need to realize the political intentions standing behind the activities of the Right. At the same time, Latino church members in the United States must recognize that ministry for this generation is political in nature; indeed, to proclaim that God chooses sides with the poor and oppressed means to freely embrace the political vocation of ministry. God is already reforming the church and society of the twentieth century through the power of God's Spirit present in the struggle waged by poor Christians in the Third World who seek a more just and dignified life. Latino Christians in the United States need to tune in to God's Spirit at work in South and Central America, in Asia and South Africa, rather than spend so much time being seduced by the Christian Broadcast Network. When the Latino church in the United States catches the reformation Spirit at work in the world, then it will be able to experience the kind of empowerment needed to create the organizational structures necessary for impacting upon white society.

Latin American Christian base communities have a great deal to teach the North American Latino church in the United States. Base communities have helped Latin American Christians struggling against oppression to go beyond strictly private and individual terms in defining faith. Personal faith is understood from the perspective of the larger social reality in which the poor live. The role of faith is to create a movement for just change that begins from the bottom. Poor Christians in Latin America are reforming the status quo church in light of a rereading of scripture that recognizes the privilege of the poor and weak in the kingdom of God (1 Cor. 1:27–28).[1]

Christian base communities have taken the Bible and organized the poor around Bible study, worship, and community works. A renewed faith perspective is taking shape within this fast-growing social movement that is attempting to reform both society and the church. Christian base communities constitute the vehicle for a new reformation in the twentieth century calling for the renewal of biblical Christianity.[2] The poor of Latin America have come to the realization that the biblical notion of the parenthood of God and the equality and relationality of humanity means opposition to inequality, injustice, and any distortion of the purpose of God's creation. For instance, in Nicaragua the forty-year reign of the Somoza family was finally halted by a revolution that was made possible by Christian participation. Christians actively engaged in the process leading to Somoza's overthrow. The levels of dehumanization to which the Nicaraguan people were subjected were understood in the context of the Christian base community to be against the will of God; hence, Nicaraguan poor Christians became part of a revolutionary process that called for the integral liberation of the oppressed based on the imperatives of the good news.[3] Salvation by God in Jesus Christ does not include the passive acceptance of a crushing social order.

The Latino church of North America in the United States might consider the usefulness of the Christian base community model in its attempt to deal with the question of social justice in the ghetto. The return to biblical Christianity characteristic of the Christian base communities is best understood in terms of the poor's reappropriation of the basic structure of the biblical story. Poor Christians in Latin America are reading the scriptures from the perspective of the oppressed. By and large, the poor know how their social, economic, political, and historical story is shared by the people of God in the Bible.[4] The poor of the Christian base communities have rediscovered a fundamental dimension of the Bible: God identifies with the oppressed and poor by choosing their side, and God actively participates in their liberation. The Latino church can learn that real fundamentalism means reading the scriptures from the perspective of the oppressed.[5]

Doing theology from the perspective of the poor enables members of the Latino, Black, and white church traditions in the United States to get in touch with the original context of the people of God whose history is recorded in the Bible. Moreover, such a theological perspective makes it possible to examine the nature of Christian action in a world whose economy is not necessarily designed to respond faithfully to the needs of suffering humanity (Matt. 25:31–46). Third World theologies of liberation are calling for the church to exercise leadership in the enormous task of transforming the very nature of the way people live together on this planet which groans for liberation (Rom. 8:22–24). The new reformation being modeled for Christians in the United States by the Christian base communities of Latin America makes it clear that the promises of God in the Bible offer personal salvation as well as social, economic, and institutional transformation. Life can be structured in such a way as to reflect the intentions of the gospel for human society and individuals.

The church often believes itself to be the center of God's activity in the world; however, its tendency to harmonize Christian ethical concerns with the American "success story" has caused many persons to seek God's presence in humanizing movements outside the boundaries created by organized Christianity. The Church of All Nations realized that one of the ways to begin wrestling with Christian action issues would be in working for humanizing change at the level of the local community. The congregation learned to see the signs of death pervading the air in both the New York ghetto and the village streets of Central America. By forming our own Christian base community, we could make real a certain level of ecclesial-social empowerment for the poor in a North American barrio. The Bible was the heart of the congregation's reconstructed faith stance.

At a conference held at New York Theological Seminary, Pablo Richard, a Chilean biblical scholar and sociologist, shared a very interesting story about a church meeting he attended in Costa Rica. The bishop who was present had apparently announced to the community that it was no longer necessary to study the Bible in the style of the base community. He argued that all Christians already know what is contained in the scriptures; any further study would simply be redundant. The official church, which has a long history of identification with the establishment, knows how radicalizing biblical literature can be. The official church would prefer poor Christians in Central America to identify with the traditional status quo.

The Church of All Nations experienced these radicalizing effects the moment it read scripture from the perspective of the oppressed. The church had formerly functioned to assimilate persons into the dominant way of thinking about life in North American society. The new way of relating to scripture led to the difficult task of disengaging faith from the legacy of the missionary past. The missionary theology on which the church was nurtured had made it possible to accept human suffering. That traditional background called for living faith "outside" history. The Christian life was no more than a private, apolitical link to a God "up there." Christian ethics was understood in terms of personal issues, centering around the suppression of pleasure. There was no room to think about Christian social action in the life of the community; indeed, scripture was read in such a way as to negate any talk of the vocation of Christian action ministry.

The Church of All Nations engaged in a process that allowed it to break out of the old wineskins. The congregation moved to establish links with grass-roots organizations engaging in social action issues affecting the life of the poor on the Lower East Side. This involved taking seriously the notion that God acts in history and takes sides with the least among us when they demand a more human life and a just social order. The deeper our congregation engaged in biblical reflection, the more committed it became to issues of justice and peace.

The Latino community can help to revitalize the Latino, Black, and white church traditions in the United States. For example, the Mexican War in the 1840s was an occasion when a Latino issue gave rise to the issue of civil disobedience as propounded by Henry David Thoreau. He went to jail because he refused to pay taxes to support the United States' expansionist war with Mexico. It is said that when Ralph Waldo Emerson visited him there, Thoreau asked him what he was doing out of jail. The Latino reality helped to give shape to the very nature of civil disobedience.[6] Thoreau's principles of civil disobedience became the basis for social justice action as practiced by such notables as Gandhi and Martin Luther King, Jr. The invisibility of the Latino community in the United States can be partly overcome by a conscious reappropriation of the Latino contribution to shaping public life and ethics since the time of Henry David Thoreau.

The voicelessness of the Latino community in the larger society has caused the rise of grass-roots organizations in sections of the country where the Latino population is very large. These organizations are now in the process of becoming social, economic, political, and cultural advocacy institutions. The Latino, Black, and white churches might consider identifying these institutions and linking their Christian action efforts to them. Establishing that kind of relationship will enrich the ecclesial reality of each of the traditions mentioned, break with the biracial structure of U.S. society, include a significant voice in the debate over public policy, and secure a greater understanding of the connection between human rights and economic justice. The Latino community offers the church the capacity to see social justice issues in terms of linking social justice action to the struggle of the poor and oppressed, not only of the Third World but of the First as well.

A Latino organization that has helped to nationalize the social and political concerns of the Puerto Rican and other Latino communities is the National Congress for Puerto Rican Rights (NCPRR). Its goals are to raise the country's level of awareness concerning the plight of Latinos, advocate the civil rights of Latinos in the United States, and focus on U.S. policy in Central and South America. On October 4, 1986, this organization held a highly successful demonstration in the nation's capital that focused on U.S. policy in Central America and the Caribbean and the concern for Latino civil rights. The protest march was described by the media as the largest Puerto Rican–sponsored demonstration in the history of the country; however, it was attended by people fairly representative of the racial and national plurality that distinguishes U.S. society. If the church (Latino, Black, and white) remains open to organizations like the NCPRR, a new stage will be reached in the attempt to develop an authentic theology of justice. It is not always necessary to go overseas to exotic lands to do theology "from below." The church can begin to do such theology at home. The church can participate in global liberation by starting to make connections at home, by joining grass-roots organizations that have arrived at a holistic understanding of oppression and liberation.

Coming Home for the New Reformation

Third World theologies of liberation have contributed to a new level of excitement within North American Christian circles. The church of the Southern Hemisphere (poor) has been busy reclaiming the Christian message. Meanwhile, like it or not, the church of the North Atlantic (rich) has been coming to the realization that poor Christians are showing the church the way into the next millennium.[7] Today, Christians in the United States are being asked to take sides with the poor and reread the scriptures from their perspective. The poor have been heard in many places within both the Catholic Church and the Protestant Church. For instance, the American Roman Catholic bishops have incorporated the concept of the option for the poor in pastoral letters issued over the last five years. The theology of those letters clearly has its background in the Latin American bishops' conferences held in Medellín, Colombia (1968), and Puebla, Mexico (1979).[8] The United Methodist Church came out with a major document focusing on peace and disarmament entitled *In Defense of Creation,* which also reflects the influence of the new theology coming from the "church of the South."

The social justice struggles of persons of color within U.S. society have been instrumental in helping the status quo church evaluate the renewing possibilities of the new theology. During the 1960s and 1970s the Roman Catholic Church experienced growth in its Latino membership, which helped it to look closely at the significance of Medellín and Puebla. The early 1980s have seen another period of growth in the Latino membership of the church. This new growth is occurring primarily within the ranks of the Catholic Church's Central American constituency. Many of the new members of the Catholic Church have come to the United States fleeing wars in Central America. They have some experience with Christian base communities and tend to be liberationist in their theology. Through them many Roman Catholic parish clergy are becoming sensitive to the concerns of liberation theology; moreover, they are discovering the biblical roots of the new theological perspective.

The Protestant Church's progressive wing has undergone a similar process of sensitization to the concerns of the poor and oppressed. Ever since the Black church became a social institution in the eighteenth century the racial morality of white society has been under assault. The Black church tradition has kept progressive Protestant Christians faithful to the scriptures by helping white society reformulate its morality and attempt to develop an authentic theology of justice.[9] In 1975 an important stage of development in the Latino, Black, and progressive white church traditions was reached with the Theology in the Americas project. Third and First World theologians gathered in Detroit to dialogue around the themes and concerns raised by liberation theology.[10] Again, the influence of the sweeping theological changes inspired by poor Christians in the Third World was evident.

National liberation movements in the Third World since the 1940s had their parallel in the United States in the 1960s in the civil rights struggle. The Latino and Black poor of the urban ghetto waged their protest against the dehumanizing effect of poverty by rioting in the streets. That historical moment made it possible for a large Black and smaller Latino vanguard to have an impact on denom-

inational structures and strike a serious blow against racism and social inequality. The militancy of persons of color
during this period caused many white progressive Christians to struggle with the new notion of doing theology
from the perspective of the oppressed. Progressive Christian publishing houses helped North American Christians
embrace and deepen their understanding of this new way
of thinking about God and the scriptures. Indeed, for
many white ministers trained in the 1950s, doing theology
from below put them in touch with the European and
North American traditions of political theology.[11]

Christianity in the United States has clearly moved to
new ground. Many Roman Catholic and Protestant Christians here have aligned themselves with the struggles of
the oppressed and poor of the Third World—especially in
Central America and South Africa. Conservative Christians have also mobilized their social forces to counteract
the solidarity efforts of the so-called liberal church. The
only way to know which group has the correct theological
understanding about God's activity in current affairs is to
examine each group's assessment of biblical religion. Only
those who do justice to the basic structure of the biblical
story can properly claim to speak for the Christian tradition on human rights, peace, justice, freedom, and love.
Christians everywhere must decide who is faithfully ex-
pounding the theological structure of the Bible. The exodus stands out as the central event of the Old Testament,
through which all events and social relations in history are
to be interpreted. Progressive Christians are standing on
secure ground by investing themselves in the new theology and its vision of a new earth (Luke 4:18–19).

The progressive church in the United States can still
strengthen its solidarity with people of color. For instance,
the white progressive church boldly took up the civil
rights struggle in the 1960s, but it has not moved very
swiftly on the struggle for economic justice. The civil
rights philosophy of the progressive white church supposed that integration into the basic structure of white
society was the final goal of the civil rights movement. The

moral virtue of an integrated society cannot be denied; however, an economic structure that continues to assure the existence of an underclass of mostly "persons of color" violates the moral consciousness.

In the 1980s, the progressive white church has taken up the cause of Central American refugees. The murder of Archbishop Oscar Romero and four churchwomen in El Salvador in 1980 caused the moral outrage that led to the formation of the Sanctuary movement. This movement, which offers refugees a haven from political oppression, has grown into a powerful instrument of Christian witness that focuses public attention on U.S. foreign policy in Central America. Human rights violations in Central America have received the bulk of attention by the Sanctuary movement. However, the fundamental issue of the dynamics of wealth and poverty governing the relationship between the United States and Central America has not been fully examined by the movement. The progressive white church's advocacy of justice for the oppressed poor of Central America living in this country as refugees still needs to include the vision which the oppressed poor themselves have of a new social order based on justice and equality.

The progressive white church too readily avoids the question of economic justice. This tendency has raised doubts about its degree of identification with the struggles of the oppressed poor for human rights and economic justice. The New Testament's image of the new social order (Acts 2:42–47; 4:32–37) tends to be left out of the social-ethical stance of the progressive white church. The basic characteristic of the Acts community was the common ownership of goods. There was not a needy person among the first Christians in Jerusalem because they shared their possessions. They did this in order to eradicate poverty within the community. Progressive white Christians have turned aside from this image of a new social order based on economic justice and communal values. Indeed, progressive white Christians have expressed great confidence in the present social order, as evidenced

by their support of liberal and reform-style government.
The people in the ghetto know that very little humanizing
change enters their lives as a result of so-called welfare
state politics. The poor in the barrio feel they are ne-
glected by the progressive white church, which advocates
the human rights of the poor and oppressed in the Third
World but seldom makes connections with the suffering
humanity in the ghettos of the United States.

Many lay and clergy teams have gone to Third World
countries to collect information about the causes of poverty and human suffering. The progressive white church
has become acutely sensitive to the reality of oppression
and dehumanization in the Third World and its relationship to the economic structures of North Atlantic nations.
However, the biracial frame of reference in U.S. society
causes the progressive white church to blame racism—a
human rights issue—for economic and social inequality.
By and large, the inequalities built into the global economic structure are left alone. The progressive white
church appears convinced that simple reform of the international economic system will create sufficient levels of
humanizing change. In other words, progressive white
Christians in the United States do not believe in changing
the basic structure of economic life in the North Atlantic
world. There may be some value in the notion of humanizing capitalism, but the poor have not been convinced of
it.

In the United States, progressive white Christians have
demonstrated outside South African consulates. They
have joined the many voices in South Africa demanding
that apartheid be dismantled in favor of a free and racially
open society. The political economy of South African society has not been equally called into question, however.
Progressive white Christians have also signed peace
pledges committing themselves to demonstrate in the
event that the United States invades Nicaragua. How
many have marched on local city governments in the
United States demanding housing for the homeless? Why
hasn't the progressive white church taken up the cause of

the poor and oppressed in the United States by protesting the inaction of Congress in this area of social policy? Why has the progressive white church remained almost completely silent while the civil rights gains of the last fifty years have dwindled? Why can't the progressive white church make the transformation of the social, political, and economic structures of the North Atlantic world its ultimate concern?

The progressive white church has not fully opposed the Christian Right's attempt to make capitalism synonymous with Christianity. The symbols of the Christian tradition are being manipulated to justify a type of political economy that has its roots in the European expansion begun in the sixteenth century. By and large, the North Atlantic world has prospered over the last five hundred years since the colonization of Latin America, Asia, and Africa. Yet the political economy of the North Atlantic has a very dark side to it. Prosperity in the North has produced massive levels of human suffering, oppression, dispossession, and death in the South. Pious capitalism has not prevented the implementation of unjust political and economic policies toward the Third World and people of color in the United States. Meanwhile, the progressive white church has chosen not to raise any questions about pious capitalism. It prefers to engage in a type of theological "tourism": that is to say, it eagerly embraces the latest Christian ethical fad. Currently the emphasis is on South African and Central American human rights concerns. Almost no attention is paid to the nature of the political economy causing the violations of the human rights of persons in the Third World, or to the impoverishment suffered by Latinos, Black, Native Americans, poor whites, Asians, the elderly, and women because of the political economy. The exoticism of the progressive white church has not yet yielded to the vision of structural and spiritual reformation being promoted by poor and oppressed Christians in the South— and their children in the North.

Christian voices in the Third World have declared that the future of the church is with the poor and oppressed.

Because they represent two thirds of the global population, theology must begin its task with their existential situation. Progressive white Christians in the United States who are seeking to be in solidarity with the vision of a new world articulated by the oppressed poor might look to the ghetto for understanding. In many respects, progressive white Christians have become the voice of the oppressed poor of the Third World in Western society; however, the poor and oppressed of the ghetto are not heard. The "church of the poor" is calling the progressive white church to follow it. An authentic theology of solidarity will include churches in the ghetto streets as well as in the village squares in the Third World. Jesus speaks to those who have ears to hear

Notes

Chapter 1: Journey to Wholeness

1. On the contributions of pietism to Protestant theology and Christian ethics see Paul Tillich, *A History of Christian Thought*, ed. by Carl E. Braaten, 2nd ed. (New York: Simon & Schuster, 1967).

Chapter 2: Hear This Cry

1. See Herbert Marcuse, *One Dimensional Man* (Boston: Beacon Press, 1964).

2. Ibid., pp. 1–18.

3. See Richie Perez, "The Status of Puerto Ricans in the United States" (Philadelphia: National Congress for Puerto Rican Rights, 1985).

4. William Ryan, *Equality* (New York: Random House, Pantheon Books, 1981), pp. 8–15.

5. See Richie Perez, "The Status of Puerto Ricans in the United States."

6. *The Washington Post,* August 25, 1987.

7. See Manuel Maldonado-Denis, *Puerto Rico: A Socio-Historic Interpretation* (New York: Random House, Vintage Books, 1972).

8. Daniel Rodriguez, *La Primera Evangelización Norteamericana en Puerto Rico: 1898–1930* (Mexico: Ediciones Borinquén, 1986), pp. 122–126.

9. See Manuel Maldonado-Denis, *The Emigration Dialectic: Puerto Rico and the USA* (New York: International Publishers, 1980).

10. Rodriguez, *La Primera Evangelización,* pp. 144–147. Also see chapter 5, "Evangelizar y Civilizar."

11. Maldonado-Denis, *Puerto Rico,* pp. 210–230.

12. See Arturo Morales Carrión, *Puerto Rico: A Political and Cultural History* (New York: W. W. Norton & Co., 1983), chapter 12.

13. See Federico Ribes Tovar, *Albizu Campos* (New York: Plus Ultra, 1971).

14. Antonio M. Stevens Arroyo, ed., *Prophets Denied Honor: An Anthology on the Hispano Church of the U.S.* (Maryknoll, N.Y.: Orbis Books, 1980), p. 340.

15. See Pablo "Yoruba" Guzman, "Puerto Rican Barrio Politics in the United States," in Clara Rodriguez, ed., *The Puerto Rican Struggle: Essays on Survival in the U.S.* (Maplewood, N.J.: Waterfront Press, 1980), p. 123.

16. Maldonado-Denis, *The Emigration Dialectic,* p. 59.

17. Ibid., pp. 60–61.

18. See Maldonado-Denis, *Puerto Rico,* p. 72.

19. Centro de Estudios Puertorriqueños, *Labor Migration Under Capitalism: The Puerto Rican Experience* (New York: Monthly Review Press, 1970), p. 104.

20. Ibid.

21. See Maldonado-Denis, *Puerto Rico.*

22. Clara Rodriguez, ed., *The Puerto Rican Struggle*, pp. 40–41.

23. Centro de Estudios Puertorriqueños, *Labor Migration Under Capitalism,* p. 241.

24. See "En los Campos de New Jersey," *De Prisa: La Revista Ecumenica,* August 1986.

25. Frances Fox Piven and Richard A. Cloward, *The New Class War: Reagan's Attack on the Welfare State and Its Consequences* (New York: Pantheon Books, 1982), p. 1.

26. Ibid.

Chapter 3: Pastoral Reflections on Hidden Dimensions

1. See F. Charles Fensham, "Widow, Orphan, and the Poor in the Ancient Near Eastern Legal and Wisdom Literature," *Journal of Near Eastern Studies* 21 (1962), pp. 129–139.

2. See J. E. von Waldow, "Social Responsibility and Social Structure in Early Israel," *Catholic Biblical Quarterly* 32 (1970), pp. 182–204. Also see Norman W. Porteous, "The Care of the Poor in the Old Testament," in his *Living the Mystery: Collected Essays* (Oxford: Basil Blackwell, 1967), pp. 143–155.

3. Thomas D. Hanks, *God So Loved the Third World: The Biblical Vocabulary of Oppression* (Maryknoll, N.Y.: Orbis Books, 1983), p. 17.

4. Von Waldow, "Social Responsibility and Social Structure," pp. 188–189.

5. See Conrad Boerma, *The Rich, the Poor—and the Bible* (Philadelphia: Westminster Press, 1979), p. 18.

6. See Edward Neufeld, "The Emergence of a Royal-Urban Society in Ancient Israel," *Hebrew Union College Annual* 31 (1960), pp. 44–45.

7. Hanks, *God So Loved the Third World,* chapter 7.

8. Neufeld, "The Emergence of a Royal-Urban Society," pp. 44–45.

9. Richard Shaull, *Heralds of a New Reformation: The Poor of South and North America* (Maryknoll, N.Y.: Orbis Books, 1984), chapter 2.

10. See Martin A. Cohen, "The Prophets as Revolutionaries: A Sociopolitical Analysis," *Biblical Archaeology Review,* May–June 1979, pp. 12–19.

11. Ibid., pp. 14–17.

12. See Shaull, *Heralds of a New Reformation.*

13. Ibid., pp. 23–25.

14. George V. Pixley, *God's Kingdom* (Maryknoll, N.Y.: Orbis Books, 1981), pp. 66–67.

15. Ibid., p. 68.

16. Ibid., pp. 69–71.

17. Fernando Belo, *A Materialist Reading of the Gospel of Mark* (Maryknoll, N.Y.: Orbis Books, 1981), pp. 81–86.

18. Pixley, *God's Kingdom,* pp. 71–87.

19. See Julio de Santa Ana, *Good News to the Poor: The Challenge of the Poor in the History of the Church* (Maryknoll, N.Y.: Orbis Books, 1979), chapter 4. Also see Gil Dawes, "Working People and the Church: Profile of a Liberated Church in Reactionary Territory," in William Tabb, ed., *Churches in Struggle: Liberation Theology and Social Change in North America* (New York: Monthly Review Press, 1986).

20. See Santa Ana, *Good News to the Poor,* chapter 5.

21. Ibid., chapter 6.

22. For the distinction between the "royal" and "prophetic" traditions see Walter Brueggemann, *The Prophetic Imagination* (Philadelphia: Fortress Press, 1978). Also see Rosemary Radford Ruether, "The Conflict of Political Theologies in the Churches:

Does God Take Sides in the Class Struggle?" in Tabb, ed., *Churches in Struggle*, pp. 18–31.

23. José Míguez-Bonino, *Toward a Christian Political Ethics* (Philadelphia: Fortress Press, 1983), p. 57.

24. Ibid. Also see José Míguez-Bonino, *Doing Theology in a Revolutionary Situation* (Philadelphia: Fortress Press, 1975).

25. Julio de Santa Ana, ed., *Towards a Church of the Poor* (Maryknoll, N.Y.: Orbis Books, 1981), p. 52. Also see Guillermo Cook, *The Expectation of the Poor: Latin American Base Ecclesial Communities in Protestant Perspective* (Maryknoll, N.Y.: Orbis Books, 1985).

26. Gustavo Gutiérrez, *A Theology of Liberation* (Maryknoll, N.Y.: Orbis Books, 1973), pp. 21–27.

Chapter 4: Transformation in the Parish

1. George Nava, director, *El Norte* (1984).

2. Anna Maria García, director, *La Operación* (1982).

3. Alfonso Beato, director, *Puerto Rico: Paradise Invaded* (1972).

4. UNIFILM, *The Heart of the Lower East Side*. Available through the Center for Puerto Rican Studies at Hunter College, New York City.

5. Don Murray, director, *The Cross and the Switchblade* (1970).

6. Manuel Maldonado-Denis, *Puerto Rico: A Socio-Historic Interpretation* (New York: Random House, Vintage Books, 1972), chapter 7.

7. Manuel Maldonado-Denis, *The Emigration Dialectic: Puerto Rico and the USA* (New York: International Publishers, 1980), chapter 2.

8. Noam Chomsky, *On Power and Ideology: The Managua Lectures* (Boston: South End Press, 1987), p. 61. Also see *The Christian Science Monitor*, April 21, 1987.

9. Carlos and Maria's situation was debated before the passage of the new Immigration Act known as the Simpson-Rodino bill, which went into effect in May 1987. The new law stipulates penalties for employers who knowingly hire an undocumented person.

10. Jenny Pearce, *Under the Eagle: U.S. Intervention in Central America and the Caribbean* (Boston: South End Press, 1983), p. 28.

11. Center for Immigrants' Rights, *A Report on the New York Public Hearing on the Plight of Undocumented Immigrants and Refugees in New York City, October 17, 1985.* Available at Center for Immigrants' Rights, 48 St. Mark's Place, New York, NY 10003.

Chapter 5: Personal Renewal

1. See Richard Shaull, *Heralds of a New Reformation* (Maryknoll, N.Y.: Orbis Books, 1984).

Chapter 6: The New Reformation: Solidarity and Connection

1. See Alvaro Barreiro, *Basic Ecclesial Communities: The Evangelization of the Poor* (Maryknoll, N.Y.: Orbis Books, 1982).
2. See Richard Shaull, *Heralds of a New Reformation* (Maryknoll, N.Y.: Orbis Books, 1984).
3. See Robert McAfee Brown's essay, "The Preferential Option for the Poor," in William Tabb, ed., *Churches in Struggle* (New York: Monthly Review Press, 1986).
4. See Thomas D. Hanks, *God So Loved the Third World* (Maryknoll, N.Y.: Orbis Books, 1984).
5. Ibid., pp. 61–69.
6. See chapter 4 in William J. Wolf, *Thoreau: Mystic, Prophet, Ecologist* (Philadelphia: Pilgrim Press, 1974).
7. See Wahlbert Bühlmann, *The Coming of the Third Church* (Maryknoll, N.Y.: Orbis Books, 1977).
8. See Tabb, ed., *Churches in Struggle.*
9. See Peter J. Paris, *The Social Teaching of the Black Churches* (Philadelphia: Fortress Press, 1985).
10. See Sergio Torres and John Eagleson, eds., *Theology in the Americas* (Maryknoll, N.Y.: Orbis Books, 1976).
11. See Thomas W. Ogletree's essay, "From Anxiety to Responsibility: The Shifting Focus of Theological Reflection," in Martin Marty and Dean G. Peerman, eds., *New Theology,* No. 6 (New York: Macmillan Co., 1969).

Suggested Reading

Barreiro, Alvaro. *Basic Ecclesial Communities: The Evangelization of the Poor.* Maryknoll, N.Y.: Orbis Books, 1982.
An excellent introduction to the Latin American base community movement. Discusses the poor's rediscovery of the Bible and the God who takes their side.

Birch, Bruce, and Larry L. Rasmussen. *The Predicament of the Prosperous.* Philadelphia: Westminster Press, 1978.
Directed especially to the North American middle-class reader, this book describes the liberation perspective from the standpoint of environmental ethics and global concerns. An important work in terms of the pedagogy of the nonpoor.

Boff, Leonardo. *Ecclesiogenesis: The Base Communities Reinvent the Church.* Maryknoll, N.Y.: Orbis Books, 1986.
A study of the Christian base community in terms of ecclesiology. Two conceptualizations of the church are related in this work—the hierarchical, exemplified in the Roman Church, and the communitarian, represented in the base communities.

Brueggemann, Walter. *The Prophetic Imagination.* Philadelphia: Fortress Press, 1978.
Sets forth the prophetic task of the church, presenting the liberation perspective in terms of the break with enculturated Christianity.

De Gruchy, John W. *Theology and Ministry in Context and Crisis.* Grand Rapids: Wm. B. Eerdmans Publishing Co., 1987.
This book discusses the meaning of the ordained ministry in the context of the South African Christian struggle against apartheid. It points to the development of a new understanding of the ministry based on concern for justice on behalf of the oppressed.

Hanks, Thomas D. *God So Loved the Third World: The Biblical Vocabulary of Oppression.* Maryknoll, N.Y.: Orbis Books, 1983.

A biblical scholar shows that the category of oppression is part of the basic structure of biblical theology. He explains how the Christian base communities and liberation theology represent aspects of a new reformation characterized by a rereading of scripture from the perspective of the oppressed poor.

Rodriguez, Daniel. *La Primera Evangelización Norteamericana en Puerto Rico: 1898–1930.* Mexico: Ediciones Borinquén, 1986.

A church historian traces the interaction of religion and politics during the United States' colonization of Puerto Rico, including the role of the Protestant missionaries in the colonial project.

Shaull, Richard. *Heralds of a New Reformation: The Poor of South and North America.* Maryknoll, N.Y.: Orbis Books, 1984.

A careful examination of the Christian base communities in the light of scriptural and theological resources. Shaull relates the story of the base communities from a Protestant perspective, indicating how they are imaging a new form of church and society. He discusses the implications of the "new reformation" for the North American Christian community.

Tabb, William, ed. *Churches in Struggle: Liberation Theology and Social Change in North America.* New York: Monthly Review Press, 1986.

A collection of essays drawn from the progressive North American church communities, showing how liberation theology contributed to social change.

Tamez, Elsa. *The Bible of the Oppressed.* Maryknoll, N.Y.: Orbis Books, 1982.

The biblical motifs of oppression and liberation are set forth in light of the reality of the oppressed poor.